To Dear M.
Lots of love
Liles, Sue + Ollie ...

NAPOLEON
BONAPARTE

POCKET
GIANTS

NAPOLEON BONAPARTE

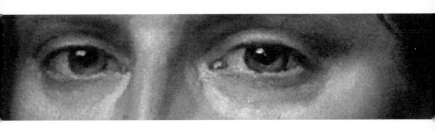

POCKET
GIANTS

WILLIAM
DOYLE

Cover image © Bridgeman Images

First published 2015

The History Press
The Mill, Brimscombe Port
Stroud, Gloucestershire, GL5 2QG
www.thehistorypress.co.uk

British Library Cataloguing in Publication Data.
A catalogue record for this book is available from the British Library.

ISBN 978 0 7509 6109 7

Typesetting and origination by The History Press
Printed in Malta, by Melita Press.

Contents

Acknowledgements

Warmest thanks to Tony for suggesting, to Mike for reviewing, and to Christine for *insisting*.

Introduction

A Giant at 5ft 6in

I am apart from everybody, I accept nobody's conditions.

Napoleon, 1806[1]

Bonaparte Family Tree

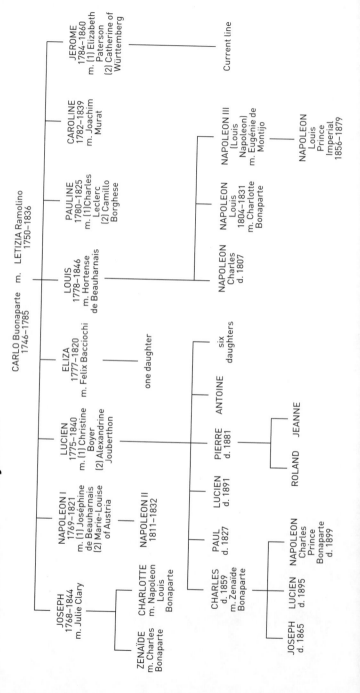

From the earliest stages of the French Revolution there were predictions that it would end in the rule of a soldier. Everybody knew about Julius Caesar, who had destroyed the ancient Roman Republic, or Oliver Cromwell who had seized supreme power in the British Isles after the execution of Charles I. Nobody was sure who the usurping general might be. Until he defected to the enemy in 1792, the most likely figure seemed to be the Marquis de Lafayette, self-styled 'hero of two worlds' who had served with George Washington in America and commanded the National Guard which policed the early Revolution. Then the threat seemed to come from Charles Dumouriez, who defeated France's invading enemies and conquered Belgium in the winter of 1792–93. But he in turn defected, and by 1795 many eyes were on Charles Pichegru, who had led a successful French invasion of the Dutch Republic. Nobody gave a thought to a young Corsican artillery officer with an ambiguous political record who found himself defending the Republic that October, the revolutionary month of Vendémiaire, in command of troops who shot down royalist rebels in Paris.

So there was widespread incredulity when 'General Vendémiaire', as Napoleon Buonaparte was now derisively known, was appointed a few months later to command the Army of Italy. He had no field experience beyond commanding units of artillery. He was short, scruffy, sallow and spotty, and he spoke French with a strong Italianate accent. The senior staff of the Army of Italy were prepared to despise him. But, despite themselves, they came away from their first meeting curiously impressed. He exuded an air of confidence and command – especially, as one said, when he put on the general's hat which would become his trademark. He promised to lead his small, neglected and undersupplied force over the Alps and into the most fertile plains on earth: 'Rich provinces, great towns will be within your power; there you will find honour, glory and riches.'[2]

Over the next year he proved as good as his word. In a series of brilliant marches and battles he defeated all France's enemies in Italy, above all the power against which war had originally been declared in 1792: Austria. The Austrians signed peace preliminaries at Leoben in April 1797, with Napoleon's army only a few days' march from Vienna. Virtually unknown only two years earlier, he had won not just the Italian campaign, but the entire war on the continent. Thus he began to change the face of Europe several years before he took power in France.

He had done it without authorisation from Paris. Under the peace terms finalised at Campo Formio in October, former Austrian territories in Italy became the Cisalpine Republic – in effect, the general's personal state. The Austrians were compensated with the territories of Venice, the oldest republic in Europe, now simply snuffed out. Some of the changes wrought by this newcomer on the international stage would prove transient, but after him Italy would never look or feel the same again. Redrawing boundaries that had been the work of centuries, the young general began to think of himself as a man of destiny. 'What I have done so far is nothing,' he told an enquirer. His intention was to be as powerful in France as he now was in Italy: 'I declare to you that I can no longer obey; I have tasted command and I cannot give it up.'[3]

As yet, however, he thought 'the pear was not ripe', and until it was he had no interest in lasting peace. On returning to France, he was given command of an army to invade Great Britain, the Republic's last remaining enemy. But he saw this as a dangerous trap and looked for a better opportunity to keep his military glory bright. Ever since his youth he had dreamt of emulating the exploits of Alexander the Great, and now he fixed his sights on Egypt. The government in Paris, the Directory, was only too glad to be rid of his threatening presence, and in the spring of 1798 allowed him to go, along with the flower of the French army and navy.

In strategic terms it was a disaster. Egypt was conquered swiftly enough, but the British navy destroyed the French fleet and left the invaders marooned. Meanwhile this unprovoked invasion of a territory of the Ottoman Empire led to a hostile diplomatic chain reaction, reigniting war in Europe. A new coalition of powers expelled the French from most of Italy and seemed poised to invade France itself. By the summer of 1799 the Republic's government was plunged into crisis. Largely as a consequence of his own adventures in the east, the general's 'pear' was now ripe. As soon as the bad news from Europe reached him, he ruthlessly abandoned his army and made a dash back to France.

Welcomed as the Republic's one undefeated general, he was rapidly recruited to front a *coup d'état* aimed at replacing an unworkable constitution. When the coup was over he refused to be sidelined. He was appointed as one of three consuls to oversee the transition to a new regime, but his military prestige and the force of his personality overawed his two colleagues from the start. Under a new constitution promulgated as 1799 ended, Napoleon officially became the First Consul, invested with supreme power. A 30-year-old soldier was now the ruler of France.

Thus the nineteenth century began with triumph for Napoleon Bonaparte (now spelling his name the French way). His exploits would dominate its first fifteen years, and the memory of them would haunt the whole of it. He began by winning the war he had done so much to prolong, but which had carried him to power. Within two years, the Austrians, Russians and even the undefeated British had made peace. Simultaneously, the First Consul made peace with the Catholic Church, which had been at loggerheads with revolutionary France since 1790. He also began to lay institutional foundations which would reinforce the legacy of the Revolution in social and economic terms. Most of the country sighed with relief.

If the representative institutions which the revolutionaries had tried to establish were now supplanted by an authoritarian government, it seemed a price worth paying for the return of order and stability.

The chief remaining uncertainty was that all this hinged on the life and energies of one man – against whom extremists plotted several assassination attempts. Napoleon, and men whose careers now depended on his authority, concluded that the only way to perpetuate his achievements was through heredity. And so in 1804 he crowned himself a monarch, the Emperor Napoleon. One contemporary at least was disgusted. This was the moment at which Beethoven, who had dedicated his 'Eroica' symphony to the hero of French republicanism, scratched out the dedication, declaring that he was nothing more than an ordinary man after all.

Napoleon's empire soon embraced far more than France. He never expected the general peace of 1802 to last, nor did he desire it. 'Nothing', he told a close collaborator almost as soon as peace was concluded, 'can sound as loud as military success. A new-born government like ours needs ... to amaze and astonish.'[4] There was nothing Napoleon enjoyed more than fighting, and he looked forward to the moment when beaten enemies would give him an excuse to beat them again. He briefly dreamt meanwhile of re-establishing the former empire of sugar and slaves in the Caribbean, which had been blighted by revolutionary upheavals. A huge expedition sent to achieve this failed, but the results were still momentous: triumphant former slaves founded the black republic of Haiti, while the vast territory of Louisiana – considered useless with few island plantations to supply – was sold off to the United States. Giving up on an American empire was to have consequences far more significant, in world-historical terms, than all Napoleon's imperial ambitions closer to home.

For ten years, however, the emperor turned Europe upside down. French domination of northern Italy, recaptured by his victory at the Battle of Marengo in 1800, was steadily extended to the whole peninsula, the south transformed into a sub-kingdom ruled by his relatives. A brilliant defeat of the combined armies of Austria and Russia at Austerlitz in 1805 opened the way for a complete reorganisation of Germany, including the end of the thousand-year-old Holy Roman Empire. Victory over the Prussians the following year at Jena led to a consolidation of French hegemony east of the river Rhine and the recreation of vanished Poland as the Duchy of Warsaw.

Napoleon's ambition now extended to control of the whole European coastline. By this means he sought to exclude British trade and so bring his most persistent but least accessible enemy to its knees through economic warfare. The policy led to the attempted occupation from 1808 of the Iberian Peninsula, with Napoleon's brother a puppet king in Madrid. The uprooting of legitimate authority in Spain and Portugal sent shockwaves worldwide, especially in the Americas (even if, thanks to British intervention and native resistance, neither Iberian kingdom was ever thoroughly subdued). When the

Austrians tried to take advantage of Napoleon's Spanish entanglement, however, he defeated them once again in 1809 at the Battle of Wagram. There followed a further redrawing of maps, and the victor took a Habsburg princess as his trophy bride. She gave him the son he longed for to perpetuate an imperial Bonaparte dynasty.

Yet Wagram was Napoleon's last victorious campaign. From this point on, his 'star' – that sense of destiny which had driven him ever since 1796 – began to fade. Having overawed the whole of Germany, in 1812 he turned the full force of his empire against Russia, with the biggest army ever assembled in Europe. The continent was drained of resources in men, money and materials to mount this assault. But most of those who invaded Russia with Napoleon never came back. Though the French reached Moscow, the Russians refused to negotiate, and eventually the invaders began a long march back as winter closed in. The retreat from Moscow is one of the most complete disasters in military history, and the whole campaign left an enduring mark in Russian historical memory. It provided the setting for Leo Tolstoy's *War and Peace*, perhaps the greatest novel ever written.

Tsar Alexander was now determined to destroy the upstart Corsican who had so brutally violated the Russian Empire; but it took another year of fierce fighting to drive the French forces out of Germany and back across the Rhine. Now Prussia and Austria grasped the chance to throw off their French oppressors and, supported by British money, allied armies crossed into France itself.

Unused to defeat, Napoleon still believed he could repel them and managed to fight some brilliant battles against the odds during the early spring of 1814. But, with Anglo-Portuguese forces also pushing up from Spain, it was clear that resistance was doomed. By the end of March the emperor's leading lieutenants were demanding that he abdicate. Surviving attempted suicide, he was humiliatingly endowed by the victorious allies with a tiny island kingdom on Elba – within sight, on a clear day, of his native Corsica.

For nearly a generation Napoleon had been the dominant figure in Europe. Almost every corner of the continent, and some repeatedly, had experienced his campaigns and the depredations of his soldiers. Between 3 and 5 million lives were lost in the course of conflicts which he had instigated or provoked. Detested and feared throughout Europe, he was also idolised by many in that Romantic age as a hero to whom ordinary rules and constraints did not apply.

His career ended with yet another episode of breathtaking boldness. After eleven months on Elba, he made a dash for France, where disillusion with the restored Bourbon regime had already set in. Soldiers he had once commanded could not bring themselves to stop his triumphant march to Paris. Napoleon claimed to be a new man, chastened by his previous experience, but the powers who had defeated him declared him an international outlaw. After a mere 100 days the army that had rallied to him was defeated at Waterloo on 18 June 1815.

Napoleon spent the last six years of his life reflecting on how he ought to have won; the Duke of Wellington, who had beaten him, admitted that it had been a close-run thing. But even if Waterloo had been another Napoleonic victory, the coalition which had taken so long to unite against him would undoubtedly have fought on until he was brought down again. The other powers of Europe recognised, from bitter experience, that there was no dealing with a warlord who never felt bound by anything that did not suit him and who had come to believe that he could always impose his will by boldness and force. The 'Corsican Ogre', as his enemies called him, was a giant who had to be locked up. And even on St Helena, a tiny isle in the midst of the South Atlantic Ocean, thousands of miles from the continent where he had so often triumphed, his vanquishers surrounded him with hundreds of soldiers and constantly patrolling warships, unable to believe even now that the remotest of exiles was enough to contain his giant presence.

1

The Revolutionary Legacy

The Revolution, despite all its horrors, has nevertheless been the true cause of the regeneration of our ways.

Napoleon, 1816[5]

Though it was often predicted, the seizure of power in France by a soldier only came about after ten years of revolution. Even then, as General Bonaparte surrounded the legislature with soldiers on 9 November 1799, not all obeyed him without hesitation. The unreliability of the army had dogged the French Revolution from the start. Nobody had trusted it in 1789. The people of Paris were terrified that the king would use troops to dissolve the self-proclaimed National Assembly and cow the capital into acceptance. That was why they had stormed the Bastille on 14 July, in a desperate search for arms to defend themselves. But mutinous soldiers had also joined the insurrection. The French Revolution succeeded because Louis XVI dared not risk sending troops he no longer trusted into the riotous city.

The next three years brought a widespread collapse of military discipline as the ranks turned against their aristocratic officers and many of the latter emigrated. Foreign rulers watched with malicious pleasure, concluding that any future conflict with France would be a walk-over. The coming of war in 1792 proved them wrong, but until 1794 the French army was fully occupied in defending the embattled Republic against external enemies and provincial rebels. There were no spare troops to police Paris, and, without reliable defenders, the National Convention was at the mercy of the revolutionary militants of the capital, the sans-culottes.

The army was transformed after 1793 by mass conscription, and by victories against both foreign and internal enemies. By 1795 the Convention felt confident enough to deploy disciplined troops against Parisian insurgents – most spectacularly in October under the command of 'General Vendémiaire'. From then on, the army and its generals were regularly involved in politics and constantly concerned that the quarrels of civilians might squander the fruits of their victories.

Those quarrels were largely about the meaning of the Revolution. It had begun when Louis XVI, an absolute monarch who shared his authority with nobody, was forced by financial collapse and bankruptcy to convoke a long-defunct representative assembly, the Estates-General. Elections throughout the spring of 1789 proved the occasion for an outpouring of grievances about the way the kingdom was governed and society organised. Yet, six weeks after the Estates convened, nothing had been achieved as the claims of commoner deputies for a voice commensurate with the numbers they represented were resisted by nobles insisting on their traditional privileges.

Non-noble frustration boiled over on 17 June when a majority of the deputies declared themselves to be the National Assembly, in effect seizing sovereignty from the king in the name of the French nation. Louis XVI was reluctantly forced to accept this – a loss he barely understood as yet. His failure to act against the rioters on 14 July saved the Assembly and vindicated its claims. Henceforth the sovereignty of the nation was accepted as the founding doctrine of the French Revolution. Successive regimes, including Napoleon's, acknowledged it whenever they made constitutional changes, rigged though the plebiscites which endorsed them might be.

The National Assembly saw its mission as giving France a written constitution. Prefaced by a Declaration of the Rights of Man and the Citizen, the constitution enshrined representative government, the rule of law, equality (of men at least) before the law, careers open to talent, freedom of thought and expression, and security of persons and property from arbitrary power. Inspired by these fundamental principles, the Assembly abolished most of the social and institutional structures that had evolved in France over many centuries and replaced them by what the deputies hoped were more rational and humane values, deriving from the enlightened thought of the decades before 1789.

Boundaries were redrawn wholesale. Administrative units were made as equal and uniform as possible. A commitment was declared – and honoured by subsequent assemblies – to produce a single nationwide decimal system of weights and measures and a uniform code of laws. Cruel and unusual punishments were abandoned. Even the death penalty was challenged, albeit unsuccessfully. (The guillotine, its new instrument, was chosen because it was swift, reliable and presumed painless and humane.)

Reforms so comprehensive could not fail to alienate those groups who lost by them. Nobles, stigmatised from the start by the fierce resistance of many of their number to the establishment of the National Assembly, soon found themselves deprived of the privileges and social advantages they had traditionally enjoyed. Increasing numbers flaunted their disgust by emigrating. In 1790 the Assembly decreed the abolition of nobility itself. (By then the term 'aristocratic' had come to mean anything contrary to the spirit of the Revolution.) Not all nobles, including the young Buonaparte, were opposed to the new order, but the antics of the émigrés left them all under constant suspicion.

Even more explosive were the Revolution's dealings with the Catholic Church. From the start, the Assembly's policy was to nationalise it. Paradoxically, this implied taking away the Church's former monopoly of public recognition and granting full toleration to other creeds. As early as August 1789 the Church was stripped of its income, and only weeks later its lands (a sixth of the country) were confiscated and put up for sale to fund the nation's debts. Monasteries were dissolved, dioceses and parishes rationalised, and the clergy transformed, under the Civil Constitution of the Clergy of 1790, into elected, salaried servants of the state. The pope was not consulted, and he made his hostility increasingly plain, leaving many clerics uncertain about accepting the reforms. Outraged at such flouting of the national will, the Assembly subjected the entire clergy to an oath of loyalty. It was stunned to find that over half refused.

The Church split, opening up the deepest wound inflicted by the Revolution. A polarised clergy meant a polarised laity. The virulence of resistance to the oath eventually cast doubt on the loyalty of even those 'constitutional' clergy who had taken it. By 1793 attempts were being made to 'dechristianise' the country entirely, and in 1795 the Republic renounced all religious affiliations. Priests were vilified as fomenters of counter-revolution, and wherever they went French armies were particularly violent towards the Church and the clergy. In 1799 the army marched on Rome and captured the pope himself. Pius VI died in France six weeks before Napoleon returned from Egypt. When the Consulate began it seemed as if the pope might have no successor.

The most spectacular casualty of religious division was the monarchy itself. There had been little or no republicanism at the outset of the Revolution in 1789, and faith in the king's good intentions only eroded slowly. The transfer, under popular pressure, of the royal family and the National Assembly from Versailles to Paris in October 1789 was intended to guarantee Louis XVI's continued co-operation with the process of reform. But, as the evolving constitution left him with ever fewer independent powers, the king realised that he had become a prisoner. When, in 1791, the pope condemned the Civil Constitution and the clergy who accepted it, the king faced a crisis of conscience. He tried to escape but was stopped at Varennes and brought back to a capital now seething with republican sentiment. His cause was not helped when foreign rulers began to threaten intervention on his behalf.

Desperate to save the constitutional monarchy it had spent two years planning, the Assembly reinstated the king and hurried its work to completion. The constitution came into operation in October with a newly elected Legislative Assembly. But when it passed laws against the émigrés and nonjuring priests, the king vetoed them. To compel him to reveal his true colours, the legislature began to press for war against the Austrians. Hoping for rescue by his wife's family, Louis XVI happily concurred, but a disastrous start to the campaign and bloodthirsty threats from the advancing enemy provoked the people to an attack on the royal palace on 10 August 1792, witnessed with incredulity and disgust by the young Napoleon. The monarchy was overthrown, and a new national assembly – the Convention – was elected to draft a constitution for a republic. It put the deposed king on trial for betraying the nation and, in January 1793, he was condemned to death.

War had brought the monarchy down. Launched with the king's fatal connivance, by the end of 1792 the war had become a republican struggle against the monarchies of Europe, with the French promising fraternity and help to all peoples struggling to recover their liberty. Few responded. Most states and their populations were appalled at the prospect of a godless regicide republic declaring open-ended war. Many French citizens were equally horrified, and in the spring of 1793 open rebellion broke out in the Vendée and other parts of western France among those seeking the restoration of Church and king. Over the summer the major cities of the south also rose up against the Paris-dominated Convention.

There followed a year of civil as well as foreign war, as the Republic struggled for survival. A low point was reached at the end of August, when the great Mediterranean naval port of Toulon surrendered to the British. It seemed that traitors were everywhere, and the Convention reacted, under sans-culotte pressure, by proclaiming a reign of terror against them. As soon as centres of rebellion were retaken, hundreds were executed in massive reprisals. At Toulon, recovered through a plan devised by artillery captain Bonaparte, there were mass shootings. Elsewhere, the guillotine left streets running with blood. Upwards of 30,000 perished in nine months, culminating in the early summer of 1794 with weeks of centralised bureaucratic executions in Paris. It was a shocking spectacle which would mar the memory of the French Revolution for ever.

The rhetoric of the Jacobins who ran the Terror, and their figurehead Maximilien Robespierre, whose downfall in July signalled its end, claimed that it was necessary to secure the survival of liberty and the egalitarian, rational and humane values that the original revolutionaries had set out to establish. Certainly the Terror's ferocity ensured that the Republic survived the crisis of 1793–94. But could the Republic work without it? 'It was terror', Napoleon later opined, 'that killed the republic.'[6]

Over the next five years, there were sincere efforts to make the Republic work. A new constitution divided executive power between five directors with an annually elected legislature of two 'Councils'. To ensure that it operated as intended, two thirds of the seats were initially reserved for members of the Convention which had produced the constitution, but monarchists, who had hoped to use free elections to restore the émigré brother of Louis XVI, saw this as a betrayal. It was a conservative uprising against the Two Thirds Law that was dispersed by Bonaparte's guns in Vendémiaire. The elections in 1797 gave further impetus to the conservative cause; within months they had to be largely annulled with the open connivance of the conqueror of Italy, in the coup of Fructidor. Nor were the elections of the next two years entirely free – or their results unchallenged by the Directory.

The events of the Revolution had, in fact, left the political nation so polarised that the electorate could not be trusted to support the republican constitution. Many, perhaps a majority, did not want a republic at all. They saw it as illegitimate – established by violence and maintained by terror – and they longed for a stability that seemingly could only be provided by a return to monarchy, priests and the consolations of religion. Although open rebellion in the Vendée had been crushed, much of western France remained disturbed by counter-revolutionary lawlessness inspired by monarchism and support for persecuted priests. Whole swathes of the south witnessed a murderous 'White Terror' targeting Jacobins who had wielded local power in the time of Robespierre.

The latter, and their sympathisers, were often called anarchists by their enemies, but at least they were republicans. Accordingly, when royalism needed to be resisted, the Directory encouraged them. Not for nothing were the months after Fructidor known as the 'Directorial Terror', with renewed persecution of priests, ex-nobles and émigrés. Jacobinism acquired a new momentum when war, which had gone so well for the Republic since 1794, once more began to go badly in the dying months of 1798. Systematic mass conscription was introduced, provoking widespread resistance and compounding rural disorder which the Directory seemed incapable of curtailing. Sinister echoes of the Terror began to be heard from old Jacobins, with calls for the persecution of nobles, émigrés and the rich in general.

By the end of the summer the crisis was abating. The armies were winning battles again, and a proposal to suspend the rule of law by formally declaring the country to be in danger was defeated. But everyone was rattled. Lurching from crisis to crisis, the Directory seemed incapable of stabilising the Republic created by the Revolution. By the time General Bonaparte returned from his heroic adventure in Egypt, he was welcomed by men seeking military support to overthrow the constitution and start afresh.

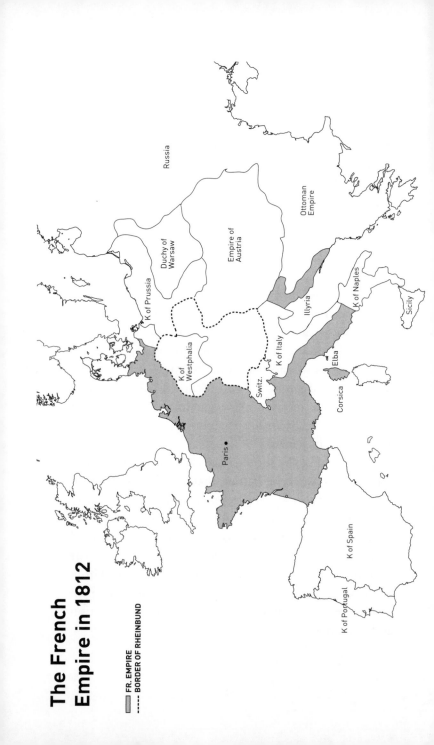

The French
Empire in 1812

FR. EMPIRE
BORDER OF RHEINBUND

Russia

Duchy of
Warsaw

Empire of
Austria

Ottoman
Empire

K of Prussia

K of
Westphalia

K of Italy

Illyria

K of Naples

Switz.

Elba

Corsica

Sicily

Paris

K of Spain

K of Portugal

2

A Corsican's Luck

That little bugger of a general scares me.

General P.F.C. Augereau, 1796[7]

Napoleon always believed in luck, and his career is unimaginable without it. He was even lucky to be French. When he was born in Ajaccio, Corsica, on 15 August 1769, the island had only been a French possession for a year, after centuries of Genoese rule. His ancestors were Italian, and he spoke Italian as readily as French. He was also lucky to be born into a noble family. The island's new French rulers set out to cultivate influential natives and arranged for the sons of Carlo Buonaparte to be educated in colleges reserved for poor nobles in France. Napoleon went to a military academy at Brienne, and then on to the Military School in Paris to be trained as an artillery officer. As a student he read widely, and as a young officer he even tried writing pamphlets and fiction. On his later campaigns he always travelled with a portable library of classics.

He felt an outsider among his French classmates, however, and his earliest political dreams were of returning to Corsica to lead an independence movement. He found regular pretexts for going back and spent four of his first six years as an officer on periodic leave in his native island. If he welcomed the coming of the Revolution it was largely because it allowed the return from exile of Paoli, the legendary leader of mid-century campaigns for Corsican freedom. But Paoli distrusted the Buonapartes, and soon enough he was quarrelling with the new regime in Paris. The young officer, who liked what the revolutionaries were trying to achieve and saw no reason to resign his commission, soon became identified with French interests. Early in 1793 his family was driven out of the island by Paolist mobs.

This too was a sort of luck. It dispelled Napoleon's ambivalence about where his loyalties lay. From this point on he began to spell his name the French way. Within the year he was proving his value as a French officer with his plan to retake Toulon. Here he had the first of many fortunate escapes, when he sustained a bayonet wound in the thigh. At the Battle of Arcola in 1796 he was almost drowned; in Paris in 1800 he avoided by seconds the explosion of an 'infernal machine' primed to assassinate him; at the siege of Ratisbon in 1809 he was hit by a spent round; at Eylau in 1807 and during the retreat from Moscow in 1812 he was almost captured by Cossacks. His escapes from Egypt in 1799 and Elba in 1815 also seemed little short of miraculous. No wonder he came to believe that a benevolent 'star' guided his destiny. He believed it of others, too: when a name came before him recommended for command, he would often ask, 'Is he lucky?'

The Revolution was a fortunate time for a young officer of talent. The emigration of so many noble officers unblocked the channels of promotion. Merely being noble could attract suspicion, but ostentatious patriotism could outweigh it. The next stage in Napoleon's progress owed much to a chance meeting with another noble-turned-revolutionary activist, Paul Barras. Sent by the Convention to oversee the siege of Toulon, Barras secured the promotion to brigadier general of the captain who planned the port's recapture – a rise which would have been unthinkable before 1789. It was Barras who gave the new general command of the troops in Vendémiaire. And then he introduced him to the widow Beauharnais, his former mistress.

The young Napoleon was a sexual innocent. It is uncertain whether he lost his virginity before 1795. He was moved to write a romantic novel, *Clisson et Eugénie*, by his admiration for Desirée Clary, whom he met in Marseille when his family fled Corsica. Her sister Julie married his elder brother Joseph. Desirée herself would later marry one of Napoleon's military rivals, Charles Bernadotte, and end up as Queen of Sweden. They lost touch when Napoleon was posted to Paris. There, in any case, he fell passionately in love with someone else. Joséphine (as he called her: her real name was Rose) Beauharnais had two children from her marriage to another general who had been executed in 1794. She was a noblewoman from the West Indies, extremely attractive by all accounts (though with bad teeth), and made her way by sleeping with men of influence. Despite his unprepossessing appearance, awkward manners and provincial tastes, the skinny young general was the man of the moment after Vendémiaire, and she cultivated him. She certainly introduced him to the joys of sex, but soon found his attentions overwhelming.

Six years his senior, she reluctantly agreed to marry him, much to the disgust of his family, who saw her as a gold-digger too old to compensate with children. They would never warm to her. And while her new husband was away campaigning in Italy and Egypt, she was persistently unfaithful. When, belatedly, he learnt the truth, his first impulse was to divorce her. Later he relented, and when he became head of state Joséphine's philanderings stopped. She became the gracious consort, then empress, an extravagant focus of fashion. Napoleon, however, while appreciating her support, never felt similarly constrained. Now he was never without women on call, and two of them bore him sons. This showed that he at least was fertile, unlike his ageing empress. Always calling himself Napoleon I, he became increasingly desperate for a legitimate heir to found a dynasty. He wanted an authentically royal consort, too. When his victory over Austria in 1809 brought the prospect of a Habsburg marriage alliance, he jumped at it and divorced Joséphine. The archduchess Marie-Louise did not disappoint him. Within a year of marriage the new empress had borne him a son, the King of Rome, known in Bonapartist tradition as Napoleon II, although he never reigned.

With four brothers and three sisters, Napoleon was a family man. Joseph as the eldest brother took precedence when their father died in 1785, but he could scarcely object later when his more successful younger sibling assumed family primacy. Among the rest, only his formidable mother commanded Napoleon's consistent respect.

Madame Mère, as she was called under the Empire, was always sceptical about her son's long-term prospects and survived him by fifteen years. Yet, as soon as he was First Consul of the Republic, he showered patronage on his relatives. When he became a hereditary emperor, he made them princes and princesses of the blood, and sooner or later most of them were given satellite kingdoms or principalities to rule in the imperial interest. Napoleon had no illusions about them. 'If I handed out crowns according to merit,' he declared, 'I would have chosen different men … I needed my family to consolidate my dynasty; … that was part of my system.'[8] And he did not hesitate to move these supposedly hereditary rulers around as it suited him. Made King of Naples in 1806, two years later the hapless Joseph was brusquely transferred to Spain, to be replaced in Italy by Joachim Murat, a general married to the emperor's sister Caroline. Napoleon's younger brother Louis, meanwhile, was given a newly created throne in Holland, only to be deposed and have his realm annexed to the Empire after only four years. It was ironic that it was Louis' son who would later revive the dynasty's fortunes as Napoleon III. Ironic, too, that Louis' wife, Queen Hortense, was the daughter of Joséphine by her first marriage.

In his difficult and quarrelsome family, Napoleon's luck perhaps failed him. But his success was based on far more than good fortune. Underpinning it all was a phenomenal capacity for hard work. He needed very little sleep, ate and drank swiftly but modestly and took copious snuff to sustain concentration. He relaxed by taking hot baths. When not campaigning, he would work a fifteen-hour day, apportioning his time rigidly. He had a soldier's respect for order and routine. Always dazzled by the heroic rulers of antiquity, such as Alexander, Caesar or Augustus, the only more recent monarchs he admired were Louis XIV and Frederick the Great, both famous for their methodical style of kingship and iron self-discipline. In this he was their equal. Though prone to repeated minor ailments and nervous tics, he was seldom impeded by them. Left-handed, he wrote very little, but dictated mercilessly for hours on end to harassed secretaries. He was notorious for stormy outbursts of anger, but people who knew him suspected that he could turn his temper on and off at will. At the same time, everybody agreed that he had formidable reserves of charm and a very winning smile – although many must have winced at his playful habit of pulling people who pleased him by the ear. He was always at his best in situations of control. Confident in addressing or reviewing large numbers of disciplined troops, he was deeply uneasy with crowds. In 1799, at the crucial moment of seizing power, a press of angry opponents left him fainting into the arms of his military bodyguards. In the summer of 1792, he had watched with horror as sans-culottes mobbed Louis XVI in his palace and later stormed it. He never forgot his first sight of slaughter – the bodies of the King's Swiss Guards, hacked and mutilated even in death by frenzied women. 'Napoleon was afraid of the people', reminisced one of his ministers, 'He dreaded insurrections.'[9] He would be less afraid, he once said, to face an army of 200,000.

Though an accomplished mathematician, Napoleon could never be trusted with numbers. He was always prepared to manipulate them to his own advantage. Enemy forces, especially when he defeated them, were inflated. So were numbers of prisoners and guns taken. French casualties were invariably downplayed. From the earliest moments of the Italian campaign which established his career he revealed himself a master of propaganda. In the reports he sent back to Paris, victories were portrayed as effortless, losses and setbacks minimised and his personal role consistently magnified. His foray into Egypt was much more chequered, but he reported it in the same relentlessly upbeat way. Napoleon only fought one battle between then and 1805, and he almost lost it. Nor did it end the war as he had intended, but Marengo was still announced as a crushing victory.

The technique was well honed by the time his Grand Army took the field in 1805. Initially its famous bulletins had undoubted triumphs to report. But later drawn or lost battles like Eylau, Aspern-Essling or Borodino, with horrific numbers of casualties, were blithely added to the list of Napoleonic victories. Men who were there at the time talked of 'lying like a bulletin', but the target of this propaganda was the public who were not there. Once in charge, Napoleon was determined to control every conduit of public information. He believed, like many of his contemporaries, that the Revolution, with all its disorder, had been brought about by irresponsible and uncontrolled scribblers. He felt the media had to be controlled by the government. Newspapers were closed down wholesale and the remaining handful compelled to toe the imperial line. All publishing was subjected to official censorship. Theatres were tightly policed. Men could not be trusted, the emperor believed, to use freedom of expression responsibly.

Nor did the propaganda end with his downfall. Napoleon was perfectly aware that the companions of his exile on St Helena were noting every word about his extraordinary career, and was sure that one day they would report his views to the world, to the detriment of successor regimes. He knew that these could not match him in glory, and he was convinced that the French loved him for it. He believed that they were easily governed by playthings and display. And so his propaganda was visual as much as verbal. He built monuments, bridges, triumphal arches, most of which can still be seen. He commissioned artists to celebrate and commemorate his appearance and achievements. Few historical figures remain more instantly recognisable. He surrounded himself with a court more glittering and formal than those of contemporary monarchs – not out of public sight at Versailles, but in the Tuileries palace at the very heart of Paris. The court grew even more lavish as the centre of an empire, inaugurated by a sumptuous coronation in Notre Dame Cathedral. And everyday life in Napoleon's capital was punctuated by showy military parades and inspections, carefully choreographed to highlight the climactic appearance of the commander-in-chief himself. The uniforms of the French armies, especially the prestigious Imperial Guard stationed in Paris, were lavish; even more so those of the generals and aides who surrounded Napoleon. It all served to highlight the modesty of his own colonel's uniform, simple grey greatcoat and famous hat decorated only with the tricolour cockade – that symbol of the Revolution without which the 'romance' of his life, as he called it, could never have happened.

3

Ending the Revolution

I said to myself: I am the one who will finish the
Revolution.

Napoleon, 1820, recalling 1796[10]

The plot of 1799, later known as the coup of Brumaire, for which General Bonaparte provided the military muscle, was born of despair that the republican constitution of 1795 could ever work properly. Its progenitor was one of the Directors, Emmanuel Joseph Sieyès, who as a pamphleteer had helped to launch the Revolution of 1789, but whose own constitutional ideas had never found the favour he thought they deserved. On the pretext that the legislature was under threat from a Jacobin plot in Paris, its two Councils were transferred to Saint-Cloud, well outside the city. Once there, the plan was to browbeat them into suspending the constitution. When they resisted, the troops moved in. A rump of deputies then meekly sanctioned a triumvirate of consuls to preside over the formulation of a new constitution.

Sieyès provided its guiding principle – 'authority from above, confidence from below' – but Napoleon brushed aside the elaborate machinery he proposed. A constitution, he later observed, should be short and obscure. That of 1799 certainly was. It was prefaced by no binding declaration of rights. It set up what all previous revolutionary constitutions, haunted by memories of old regime 'despotism', had sought to avoid: a strong central executive. It acknowledged national sovereignty, the Revolution's founding principle, by giving every male citizen a vote, and by having the whole document (retrospectively) approved in a carefully rigged plebiscite. But representative government was the main casualty. All the electorate could vote for were lists of men, from among whom the government would choose members of two chambers, the Tribunate and the Legislative Body. The integrity of the constitution was subject to the oversight of a Senate, but its members too were nominated, not elected. It was, therefore, barefaced effrontery when the consuls proclaimed that the constitution was 'founded on the true principles of representative government', much less that the Revolution was 'established upon the principles which began it'. And to claim, in conclusion, that the Revolution was over was more an expression of hope than achievement. The task facing the new First Consul was to fulfil that hope, and to prove himself more than what British Prime Minister Pitt disdainfully referred to as 'this last adventurer in the lottery of Revolutions'.[11]

The great wounds inflicted on France by the revolutionary experience still gaped open. The most pressing was war, which had already gone on for eight years and had intensified during Napoleon's absence in Egypt. The immediate threat to the Republic from foreign invasion had been lifted, but the European coalition provoked by the Egyptian adventure was still holding together, and almost all of the Italian conquests of 1797 had been lost. The war-weariness of the population was compounded by increasing tax demands, requisitions and the conscription law of 1798. There was also economic chaos following the collapse of the revolutionary paper currency, and disruption of trade through British control of the seas.

The First Consul launched immediate public appeals to enemy monarchs to make peace. He struck a conciliatory note for propaganda purposes, but energetic military preparations ordered at the same moment showed what response he expected. Nor did he himself want peace at any price: he wanted peace with victory. He was lucky that Russia, disillusioned with its allies, was now turning away from the coalition. He could concentrate all French armies against a weakened Austrian enemy, moving on Vienna simultaneously through Germany and Italy. That had been the plan in 1796, and he aimed to repeat his triumphs by leading a lightning campaign south of the Alps.

It began well with a crossing of the mountains that took the enemy by surprise. But when battle was joined at Marengo in June 1800 the French nearly lost. Only an unexpected Austrian request for an armistice enabled Napoleon to claim a great victory. And there was no march on to Vienna: the victor, in what would become a reflex action for him, hurried back to Paris to reap the political benefits. The Austrians fought on, and the knockout blow was only struck in December, at Hohenlinden – and by a rival general, Victor Moreau, who was never employed again and was destined to die thirteen years later in Germany, fighting against his old rival.

Characteristically, France's new ruler claimed all the credit for the ensuing peace, which finally achieved war aims that had been formulated as early as 1793: recognition by Austria of a French 'natural' frontier on the Rhine and the loss to France or her satellites of Habsburg territories in Belgium and northern Italy. Peace on the continent left Great Britain fighting on alone. British forces expelled the remnants of the French army from Egypt but war-weariness was as pervasive across the Channel as in France, and a new ministry in London opened negotiations. The result, in the spring of 1802, was the Peace of Amiens, in which France made promises while Britain returned all overseas possessions it had captured from the Republic. The wars of the French Revolution were over. For the first time in a decade, all Europe was at peace. Put another way, France had imposed humiliating terms on all its enemies.

The triumph was celebrated on Easter Sunday 1802 with a lavish Te Deum in Notre Dame, announced by the pealing of church bells all over Paris – the first time they had been heard since 1793. This service was deliberately planned to mark not only peace with foreign enemies, but also peace with the Catholic Church. The quarrel with Rome was the earliest and deepest divide inflicted on France by the revolutionaries. The religious issue had torn the nation apart, driven the king to take flight, inspired counter-revolutionary rebellions and led to a massive and much disputed redistribution of property. Although the Convention had sought to draw a line under the excesses of dechristianisation after the Terror by renouncing religious affiliations, religious troubles kept resurfacing, usually in alliance with royalist uprisings. On the eve of the 1799 coup they had seemed to be getting worse. The death of the captured pope in France further compounded the problem.

Napoleon had no religious faith, and in unguarded moments he gloried in the fact. But he had learnt, in negotiations with the papacy in 1797, that the Church could be surprisingly flexible in the temporal sphere, and he recognised the depth of commitment which religious faith inspired. He also saw religion as the firmest social cement. The vacant papacy afforded an opportunity for a new start, and at once Napoleon ordered funeral honours for the still-unburied Pius VI, knowing that a conclave was by then sitting (albeit under Austrian auspices) in Venice to choose a successor. The eventual election of Pius VII in March 1800 was encouraging: in 1797 he had notoriously preached accommodation with the invading French.

Sweeping back into Milan a few days before Marengo, Napoleon had convoked the city's clergy to the cathedral and assured them that the religious policy of the French Republic had been misguided. 'As soon as I am able to confer with the new pope,' he declared, 'I hope to have the happiness of removing every obstacle which still hinders complete reconciliation between France and the head of the Church.'[12] Even before the battle he had put out feelers. After it he made more determined approaches, and by August secret negotiations had begun. They went on until July 1801. At several points they almost broke down; Napoleon said they were the most difficult he had ever undertaken. Few of his closest circle thought they could succeed, or even that they should. But in the end they produced a Concordat which restored open religious worship in France with the full support of the state. However violent the two men's later quarrels were, Pius VII always acknowledged Napoleon's role in the 'restoration of the altars' and in the re-establishment of his own spiritual authority.

The Church gained little else. It had to accept toleration for other faiths and recognise that Catholicism was simply the religion of the majority in France. It had to accept that monasticism would not be restored, nor its lost lands. The state would pay clerical salaries and would appoint all bishops and priests. The pope would simply confer spiritual powers. To close the deal, he was obliged to dismiss all existing bishops, jurors and nonjurors alike, and to accept the reappointment to a new bench of some who had defied his predecessor and taken the oath of 1790. Moreover, when the agreement was promulgated, he was appalled to find attached to it an unagreed schedule of 'organic articles' which made direct contact with Rome by the French clergy almost impossible. Nevertheless, nothing did more to sew up the wounds of the Revolution. By accepting the Concordat, the papacy condoned most of what it had condemned a decade earlier – including, crucially, the loss of Church lands. For the first time, acquirers of that sixth of the country confiscated from the Church in 1789 could feel secure in their gains. Napoleon regarded this guarantee as fundamental to his regime and, at his imperial coronation in 1804, he solemnly swore to uphold it. The Concordat also shattered the alliance between the Church and the Bourbon dynasty which had underpinned so much counter-revolutionary action. God's favour had now been transferred from the sons of St Louis to the heirs of a once godless revolution; faith could no longer be invoked to justify resistance to the new government, much less attempts on the life of its head.

The most spectacular attack on Napoleon had nearly succeeded when the negotiations with Rome were still secret. On 24 December 1800 a huge explosion missed the First Consul's coach by moments. It was the culmination of a series of assassination plots. Napoleon was convinced, or professed to be, that it was the work of Jacobins and former terrorists. He used the occasion to round up and exile 130 men 'for all they have done and all they still might do'. Nine were executed. This marked a spectacular and convenient public end to the supposed Jacobin menace which had been the ostensible excuse for the coup of Brumaire.

The attempted assassination had, however, come from the opposite political extreme, as the omniscient police minister and former terrorist Joseph Fouché was quickly able to prove. Until the Concordat became public knowledge, royalism was an altogether more serious and widespread threat to the new regime. Sentiment turned bitter as realisation dawned that the general now in power had no intention of making way for a restored monarchy.

Popular royalism had always been closely linked with resistance to conscription. When new conscription laws were introduced in 1798, western districts that had never been fully pacified after the defeat of the Vendée rebellion witnessed a fresh flare-up of open revolt. A similar outburst of Catholic fervour also swept some newly incorporated Belgian departments.

During the first weeks of the Consulate, large tracts of western France slipped beyond the control of depleted local garrisons. Initially the First Consul offered conciliation. He held secret meetings under safe conduct with western rebel leaders. 'Say firmly to your fellow citizens', he told them, 'that no more revolutionary laws will devastate the fair land of France, that the Revolution is finished.'[13] A general proclamation to the western departments conveyed the same message but was followed in the first weeks of 1800 by an order to show no mercy to rebels who did not lay down their arms. By mid February most had. Captured intransigents were shot out of hand. But not all had given up for good. One of the fiercest peasant leaders, Georges Cadoudal (universally known simply as 'Georges'), came away from a stormy meeting with the First Consul determined to continue the struggle in secret. He was scarcely involved with the December plot, but heavily implicated in a number of others, even after the Concordat became public.

Rural royalism shaded into much more widespread disorder and 'brigandage'. Nowhere under the Directory were the roads entirely safe. Vendettas going back to the time of the Terror or were endemic throughout the south, and all acquirers of land confiscated from the Church, from émigrés and from victims of the guillotine were particularly vulnerable. In the popular mind, revolution had come to mean endless disorder and insecurity.

The First Consul understood this well, and from the start his rule was marked by a determined campaign throughout the country to reimpose public authority. The release of military units from foreign service strengthened his arm: they were deployed ruthlessly. In many areas justice was entrusted to military commissions with extraordinary powers. Such measures intensified after the bomb plot of 1800 into what some called the 'Consular Terror'. Special tribunals exempt from normal judicial procedures were set up in many parts of the country. Between 1800 and 1802 almost 3,000 death sentences were passed. This total was low compared with the Terror of 1793–94, and to most people it seemed a small price to pay for the return of law and order after a dozen years of chaos and uncertainty. None of it was the achievement of the First Consul alone, but few believed it could have been done without his drive and determination. Nor could they believe that the Revolution would really be over unless he remained there to guarantee it.

4

Building a Future

The fault of the Revolution is to have demolished much and constructed nothing, everything still remains to be done.

Napoleon to Talleyrand, 1797[14]

With the war won, peace with the Church, and internal disorder receding, the outstanding problem left from the revolutionary upheaval was the uncertainty of central authority. Millions hoped for a monarchical restoration, and in February 1800 the pretender Louis XVIII wrote France's new ruler a flattering letter urging him to use his authority to bring back the legitimate dynasty. Bonaparte neglected to reply until several months after Marengo, brusquely declaring that there was no hope of that. So how could an alternative future be secured? 'Everything has been destroyed,' the First Consul declared in 1802, 'it is time to create afresh. There is a government, powers, but what is everything else in the nation? Grains of sand … we must look to the future … We can do it, but we have not, and we shall not, if we do not lay upon the ground of France some masses of granite.'[15]

Only his own life, Napoleon claimed, stood between the new stability and a relapse into revolutionary anarchy. Under the constitution the First Consul held office for ten years, indefinitely re-eligible, but this offered insufficient guarantee of stability. Over the course of that triumphant spring a campaign of hints was orchestrated that the nation should show some extra token of its gratitude. The

Senate responded by proposing an automatic decade's extension to the office of First Consul. This was not at all what was intended; instead, a new plebiscite was summarily ordered on whether to extend the term for life. As in 1799, an impressively overwhelming majority was engineered in Napoleon's favour. There was now in effect a republican monarchy.

The danger of assassination was diminished after the Concordat and peace with Britain deprived the royalist cause of much of its support. But when war resumed in 1803 a new conspiracy was launched with British connivance. Early the next year it was discovered that Cadoudal was in Paris attempting to recruit Moreau – the hope of all who hated Bonaparte – into a plot to kidnap and kill the First Consul, while an unspecified Bourbon prince proclaimed the restoration of Louis XVIII. The plan was thwarted by mass arrests: Cadoudal was executed and Moreau exiled. Most spectacularly of all, Napoleon personally authorised a counter-kidnap of the only Bourbon prince within reach, the Duke d'Enghien, living just across the Rhine in Baden. He was brought to Paris, tried by a secret military court and summarily shot. Napoleon regarded Bourbon complicity in plotting against his life as a blood-feud, and this was his response. It re-emphasised his revolutionary credentials, but scarcely his republican ones. In fact, the crisis led to the final establishment of a new hereditary monarchy. Napoleon would not become a king. He would become something even greater, an emperor. Later endorsed by yet another plebiscite, the proclamation of

Napoleon Bonaparte as hereditary 'Emperor of the French Republic' took place in May 1804. As Cadoudal (in prison, awaiting trial) wryly put it: 'I have done better than I could have wished. I wanted to give France a king, and I've given her an emperor.'[16]

As the regime grew more monarchical, it became less parliamentary. Napoleon had always despised political assemblies as talking-shops for lawyers and 'ideologists'. He hoped that members nominated to the Tribunate and Legislative Body created in 1799 would be grateful enough to do as they were told. Most were; but government by assemblies since 1789 had fostered the belief that they existed to make laws and if necessary reject them. Napoleon saw no point in this. For him, the legislature was there to endorse legislation already discussed and refined in the Council of State.

During the first years of the Consulate, the chambers were bombarded with new measures. Hardly any were rejected, but many, such as the Concordat, the restoration of colonial slavery, and various aspects of the new civil code of laws, were opposed in their passage by vocal minorities, to the First Consul's increasing irritation. Finally in 1802 all pending legislation was withdrawn and advantage taken of ambiguities in the constitution to 'renew' membership of the Tribunate and Legislative Body by selecting the regime's most vocal critics for retirement. This task was entrusted to the Senate.

Originally conceived as a constitutional watchdog staffed by elder statesmen, Napoleon's Senate was increasingly used to promulgate laws in the form of 'consultations' (*senatus consultum*) beyond the competence of the legislature. Virtually a new constitution was introduced by this means in the summer of 1802 to incorporate the Life Consulate, drastically reducing the size of the Tribunate and circumscribing its procedures. The latter's last moment of defiance was when a handful of members denounced the establishment of the Empire, but thereafter it withered away until formally abolished (by *senatus consultum*) in 1807. 'In the Tribunate,' Napoleon later declared, 'they did nothing but make revolution, so I put them in order.'[17]

For some years, the emperor kept up parliamentary pretence, with ceremonial state openings, but sessions grew shorter and shorter, and between 1810 and 1813 the Legislative Body did not meet at all. Only at the very end of 1813 was it summoned again, during the Empire's final crisis – and then, at the first hint of criticism, it was suspended. When it next met, three months later, to endorse the end of the Empire, the Senate had already taken control of the process.

The constitution of 1802 abolished the 'lists of confidence' of potential deputies and officials. No longer elected, they were now simply the 600 highest taxpayers in each department. These were the core of the 'notables' of the Napoleonic regime, the social 'granite masses' intended to underpin its stability. In total they numbered perhaps 70,000 in France, and 100,000 at the height of the Empire when it took in many Italian, German and Dutch territories. They were above all landowners. Many had bolstered their wealth with land confiscated from émigrés and victims of the Terror as well as from the Church.

Although the constitution of 1799 declared all listed émigrés perpetually banished, Napoleon made open efforts almost immediately to lure them back. His aim was to reconcile them with the new regime and to recruit as many as were willing to his ruling class of notables. Over the first year of the Consulate official lists of émigrés were closed, and in 1801 a general amnesty was proclaimed for all who would pledge loyalty to the regime (and implicitly accept their losses). Thousands returned on these terms, and those whose lands remained unsold got them back. Many others recovered what they had lost by repurchase or imaginative subterfuge, but they had to recognise that new owners could not be dispossessed. That done, they were welcomed without further question into the hierarchy of Napoleonic notability, and if they served the state zealously they could expect to be further rewarded.

The year 1802 saw the introduction of the Legion of Honour. Defended by the First Consul against critics as an entirely republican order of distinctions for public service, the legion rapidly evolved after 1804 into a pillar of imperial society. By the end of the Empire it numbered over 38,000 – mostly soldiers, but also the more prominent civilian servants of the Empire. By then, too, the legion was complemented by a much more exclusive titled hierarchy of princes, counts, barons and knights introduced in 1808. It was not so much a recreation of the pre-revolutionary nobility as an attempt to supplant its lingering prestige with that of a much more meritocratic elite. Nor were these titles hereditary unless underpinned by substantial wealth: Napoleon only wished to be served by rich men. The new hierarchy succeeded, however, in attracting hundreds of old nobles, including returned émigrés. Perhaps a fifth of the 3,600 titles created went to men already noble, which Napoleon welcomed as contributing to a wider process of amalgamating pre- and post-revolutionary elites. After his downfall the returning Bourbons recognised these new titles as authentically noble, whoever held them. They also accepted the Legion of Honour as the supreme recognition of public service – as have all French regimes since.

Property owners were reassured by an even more enduring achievement: the Civil Code. Codification of French laws had been under sporadic discussion for centuries. The revolutionaries committed themselves to speeding up the process, but produced only drafts. A key figure in this was Jean-Jacques-Régis de Cambacérès, a former magistrate and member of the Convention who emerged as Second Consul in 1799 and remained a central figure in Napoleonic government until the end. Drafts made by him several years earlier were examined by his senior colleague as soon as the Consulate began. He found them to be a model of clarity. The drafts were passed to a commission of jurists at whose working sessions the First Consul often made a point of appearing and intervening, and under this pressure a preliminary version was produced for public discussion by the end of 1801. Criticism in the Tribunate impeded its passage into law, but after the purge of 1802 there were no further obstacles, and the Civil Code of the French was inaugurated a few weeks before the proclamation of the Empire. In 1807 it was renamed the Code Napoleon, and the emperor claimed, not unfairly, that it would prove his most enduring monument, far outliving his military achievements.

Napoleon's own input had been substantial – usually to make the Code more conservative. The Code produced clear and uniform rules for the holding and transmission of property, marriage and inheritance. It guaranteed all children a share in parental goods but, at Napoleon's insistence, it made women subordinate to men in most circumstances, including control of property and access to divorce. Subsequently other codes of criminal and commercial laws were issued. A determined effort was also made to universalise the decimal and metric weights and measures first decreed in 1795, but popular resistance was acknowledged in 1812, when parallel use of traditional denominations was formally permitted. Popular conservatism was positively embraced in 1806 with the abandonment of the republican calendar which had been in force since 1793, with its confusing month names and anti-religious ten-day weeks.

Responsibility for imposing and enforcing these policies throughout French territory lay with the prefects. Napoleon retained the revolutionary division of the country into roughly equal departments, but each was now to be administered not by elected bodies but, rather, by an omnicompetent nominee answerable to the central government. It was an almost instinctive return to the intendants of the pre-revolutionary monarchy. The Concordat Church operated on the same grid, its bishops often called 'prefects in purple'.

A uniform countrywide system of elite education was also launched, for notables of the future, mostly sons of existing ones, to be taught in *lycées* organised like military cadet schools. A celibate corps of teachers delivered a national curriculum of traditional Latinate letters, mathematics and science, laid down from 1808 by the University, a monopoly licensing authority.

The spirit of all these institutions, inherited from a revolution which had planned far more than it ever succeeded in establishing, was rationalisation and uniformity. Neither could be achieved, Napoleon and his collaborators were convinced, without the impulsion and backing of strong central authority. Subsequent regimes accepted the results, and the structures of Napoleonic centralisation in administration and education lasted, little changed, down to the later twentieth century.

Napoleon's proverbial luck was not confined to his personal circumstances. Underpinning all his state-building was an unprecedented ten-year run of good harvests which kept economic conditions stable after the wild fluctuations of the preceding revolutionary decade. Paper money which, through overprinting, had brought roaring inflation, had been abandoned by the time he came to power. The state's debts, which had precipitated the Revolution in the first place, had been largely liquidated by a ruthless bankruptcy in 1798, so that Napoleonic rule could be financed by taxation and the exploitation of conquered territories rather than by extensive renewed borrowing. Even the Bank of France, set up within weeks of the Consulate's establishment, had been in the planning stage before the coup of Brumaire, as had the franc, the new unit of currency first decreed in 1795. Napoleon's contribution was to give solid and consistent state support to these projects, ensuring that the bank, and the 'germinal franc' whose weight in silver was fixed in 1803, survived his regime for the best part of two centuries.

5

Napoleonic Wars

The most essential quality in a general-in-chief is
solidity of character and determination to win at
all costs.

Napoleon, 1817[18]

Napoleon owed everything to his exploits on the battlefield. He was never happier than when at the 'head of the army', and he died with those words on his lips. The one quality which he always admired unreservedly was courage under fire. He liked to portray himself as an instinctive military genius – 'You engage, and then you wait and see' – but he was a meticulous planner who had been thoroughly trained in pre-revolutionary military schools.

Humiliation in the wars of the mid-eighteenth century had led the French army to reappraise its tactics, equipment and organisation, but the years before 1789 had offered no occasions for the innovations to be tested in action. Napoleon's generation of soldiers was the first to have that opportunity. His spectacular string of victories was in many ways the vindication of old regime military reformers. He used their tactical innovations, opening battles with swarms of lightly armed skirmishers and making lines of musketry secondary to a rapid redeployment of infantry into dense columns, the so-called 'deep order', for a shock onslaught at the enemy's weakest point.

Trained as an artillery officer, he preceded assaults with massive barrages from a lighter and more manoeuvrable range of guns introduced in the 1780s. His armies were organised into self-contained divisions combining infantry, cavalry and artillery who could march and operate separately, but were trained to merge quickly for battle. From 1805, divisions were grouped into larger corps operating in the same way. And these forces lived off the land, dispensing with the huge and burdensome baggage trains which had slowed down all pre-revolutionary armies.

The armies implementing these innovations had been transformed by the Revolution. Gone was an officer corps monopolised by noblemen. The mass emigration of disillusioned officers in the early 1790s opened promotion to many talented lower ranks who could never have risen before: men like Ney, Murat, Masséna, Soult, Lannes, Bernadotte, Junot, Lefebvre – all future imperial marshals. Promotion now depended on military merit rather than seniority and privilege. Napoleon himself, though an officer, could not have hoped to rise far under the old order.

Nor were the ranks any longer made up of desperate volunteers, mercenaries and social misfits. Napoleonic warfare relied overwhelmingly, as did the armies of the Republic from 1793 onwards, on conscripted men. Military service was now deemed an obligation of citizenship and, drawing on the largest population in Europe outside Russia, it gave France a massive advantage in numbers. The *levée en masse* of 1793, which conscripted over 700,000 men, enabled the Republic to survive the crisis of its first two years. During the renewed emergency of 1798, the Jourdan Law made all single men between 20 and 25 liable for military service. Under Napoleon the full force of the state was deployed against draft-dodging and desertion, with ever-heavier demands during the last years of the Empire, and enforced service beyond a notional five years.

The triumphant campaigns of 1805–07 took a heavy toll on the magnificently trained Grand Army which fought them, and the conscripts who filled the gaps lacked the preparation their predecessors had had. Accordingly, later campaigns relied more on weight of numbers than operational skill. Napoleon's adversaries were inevitably forced to swell their own ranks in response, and the last stages of the Napoleonic wars were fought by the largest armies ever seen in Europe. Whereas the army of Italy with which Napoleon made his name in 1796–97 numbered 37,000, at his greatest triumph at Austerlitz nearly a decade later he commanded 73,000. He took over 600,000 into Russia in 1812, and at the Battle of the Nations at Leipzig in 1813 the total number of troops on a single vast battlefield was over half a million.

Napoleon's own operational innovations, built up from his personal experience, were modest. He pioneered the division of his forces into corps. He established an Imperial Guard of elite regiments, recruited from veterans who had distinguished themselves, who acted as a permanent reserve in all campaigns. He seldom had to commit them; when they were deployed in the last stages at Waterloo, their unexpected retreat before British fire marked the turning point of the battle.

This failed onslaught had been preceded by several frenzied cavalry charges, for Napoleon believed that 'without cavalry, a battle has no result.' Used as a weapon of shock, as at Marengo, the cavalry could turn a battle, and they were invaluable in decimating a fleeing enemy, or unprotected infantry. But accurate gunfire from foot soldiers formed into squares could devastate cavalry, who were extremely expensive to train and replace. Beginning with massive losses in Russia, Napoleon's last campaigns were crippled by a growing shortage of horses, whereas his Russian adversaries were able to maintain a constant supply.

Napoleon believed in swift knockout blows. He scorned defensive tactics. War for him was a matter of seeking out the enemy's main force and destroying it in a decisive battle. 'If you look through his campaigns,' observed Wellington, 'you will find that his plan was always to try to give a great battle, gain a great victory, patch up a peace, such a peace as might leave an opening for a future war, and then hurry back to Paris.'[19]

This reflex was partly political. Napoleon was never sure that his absence, and the risks he took in the field, would not produce conspiracies against him – as they did in 1808 or more seriously in 1812. Even when established as a hereditary emperor, he felt a compelling need to keep winning spectacularly. His amazing record of victories reflected the personal qualities that made him a great commander. Whenever he had the opportunity, Napoleon insisted on careful training and preparation. The Grand Army which successively humiliated the Austrians, Prussians and Russians between 1805 and 1807 was the fruit of two whole years of active encampment on the coast opposite England, ostensibly threatening a cross-Channel invasion. When it marched south into Germany to confront the forces of a new coalition, the Grand Army travelled at dazzling speed. Whether in marches or battle, Napoleon always moved faster than his opponents, maximising the element of surprise. Then, having forced his enemy to give battle, his instinct was always to try to turn the enemy's flank and reveal a weak spot in his dispositions on which to concentrate overwhelming force, first by artillery and then by the shock of massed columns and cavalry.

Napoleon always kept a substantial body of men in reserve and seldom divided his own forces. It was almost disastrous when he did so, at Marengo or Eylau, and fatal at Waterloo. Analysis of his other battles brings out any number of potentially dangerous mistakes, but Napoleon's proverbial luck furnished him with opponents incapable of exploiting them. They lacked his relentless and imaginative aggression. And so the tally of his victories mounted, and his ruthless control of propaganda minimised his setbacks. His men came to believe that he could not lose; and Wellington opined that his very presence on the battlefield was worth 40,000 men.[20] Of the sixty battles Napoleon boasted of fighting, he did indeed only lose eight (Acre 1799, Aspern-Essling 1809, Maloyaroslovets 1812, Leipzig 1813, Arcis, Laon, La Rothière 1814, and Waterloo), and drew perhaps two more that he chose to call victories (Eylau 1807 and Borodino 1812). On the other hand, he lost the last four of his twelve campaigns and abandoned two more (Egypt and Spain) for others to lose.

Napoleon's style of warfare brought brilliant success against armies of rulers who tried to confront him head-on but recognised when they had been beaten. These tactics did not work in 1812 against Tsar Alexander, whose generals kept postponing battles as they drew the invader even further into Russia, and who refused to make peace even after the capture of Moscow. Nor did Napoleon's approach work against hostile populations deprived of governments with legitimate authority to commit them, such as the people of Spain, on whom he imposed the monarchy of his own brother, Joseph, in 1808. The undisciplined guerrillas of Spain could not be defeated with a knockout blow, and their British and Portuguese allies under Wellington repeatedly withdrew into defensive positions in Portugal rather than risk an all-or-nothing clash.

Crucially, except for a few brief months in 1808, Napoleon was not in the Iberian Peninsula in person. King Joseph was no warrior, the French generals propping him up often did not co-operate easily among themselves and were not the emperor's equals as commanders. 'If Boney had been there,' confessed Wellington after victory over Masséna at Fuentes de Oñoro in 1811, 'we should have been beat.'[21] Napoleon recognised soon after it began that his Iberian incursion had been a mistake, but he could not bear to be seen to have failed. And so the 'Spanish ulcer' continued to bleed men and resources throughout the last six years of his Empire.

Iberia also offered a continental foothold for the British, quite the most inaccessible of Napoleon's enemies. For all the show of the training camps at Boulogne in 1803–05, invasion of the British Isles was never seen by him as a serious prospect. Without complete and sustained command of the sea, the enterprise was too risky. The vigilance of the British navy was not infallible, and the French were capable of daring sorties – as when General Bonaparte and an entire army were transported to Egypt in 1798. But British naval superiority was overwhelming, and only by combining with the Dutch or Spanish fleets could France hope to approach parity.

Repeatedly between 1797 and 1807 the British destroyed French or allied fleets. They maintained a steady blockade of French-controlled coastlines, while keeping their own forces in Spain, Portugal and Sicily fully supplied. Napoleon continued to build warships, even after the catastrophic defeat of Trafalgar in 1805, but his naval power was broken. It was a military stalemate: France dominated the continent, Britain ruled the waves.

Napoleon's response was economic warfare – to exclude British exports from continental markets by controlling the entire European coastline either directly or through his satellites and allies. For some years this brought serious disruption to the British economy. Between 1805 and 1812 this became the Empire's guiding strategy, driving imperial expansion in Italy, Spain, the Netherlands and north Germany, and underpinning a three-year alliance with Russia. Russia's withdrawal from the system in 1810 marked the beginning of the end for the Napoleonic adventure, even if the final trauma took four more years of fighting on an unprecedented scale.

Never before had so much of Europe witnessed such substantial destruction. Only the British Isles and remoter parts of Scandinavia and the Balkans avoided the tread of Napoleon's armies. Wherever they, and increasingly their opponents, went, they lived off the land, devastating the countryside for many miles either side of their route. Civilians who resisted their demands faced savage reprisals. The scale of misery and carnage experienced by host populations is almost impossible to calculate. Even figures for military losses in battle are notoriously approximate. What is certain is that they grew along with the growth in armies. Eleven thousand soldiers fell at Marengo; nearly 70,000 were lost or captured in the Wagram campaign nine years later. Of the 600,000 taken into Russia by Napoleon in 1812, only around 50,000 returned, and the retreating invaders left perhaps 300,000 Russian dead behind them.

For France the wars of the Empire brought death to almost 900,000 men – nearly as many people as were born in the country each year. Relatively few died in battle; nine tenths perished later from wounds or disease. Napoleon was untroubled by battlefield losses. One night in Paris, he reportedly quipped, would make them up. But he was genuinely appalled at the slaughter of Eylau, where he was nearly captured and had losses of perhaps 25,000. He recognised soon enough that casualties on this scale might be the price of continuing to dominate Europe. 'A man like me', he yelled at Metternich as the Austrian minister offered him humiliating peace terms in 1813, 'doesn't give a fuck for the lives of a million men!'[22]

6

Upending Europe

Napoleon was not a personality, but a principle.

Duke of Wellington, 1837[23]

R. RHINE

ALPS

PYRENNEES

Historic frontiers
'Natural' frontiers

French frontiers
1789–1802–1814

In France, Napoleon was a builder. In the rest of Europe, he was a destroyer. The Revolution swept away the old regime in France but, despite the bombast of its leaders and the efforts of its armies, it made few incursions beyond France's self-proclaimed 'natural' frontier of the Rhine and the Alps – until General Bonaparte burst into Italy in 1796.

Italy never recovered. Every established state or territory in the peninsula was reconfigured or disappeared between 1797 and 1810. By then only Sicily and Sardinia were not under direct or indirect French rule. Even the papacy, the oldest monarchy in Europe, was expelled from Rome, and a second pope became a French captive until 1813. Meanwhile the peace with Austria which resulted from Napoleon's Italian campaigns began a process which, over nine years, brought the dissolution of the thousand-year-old German Reich, the Holy Roman Empire. The defeated emperor was forced to accept French annexation of the Rhine's left bank. To compensate him and other secular rulers for their losses there, all the old, ecclesiastical principalities were dissolved in 1803 and their territories redistributed.

After Austria was once more defeated at Austerlitz, the old palimpsest of the Reich, with its innumerable tiny principalities, was consolidated into a handful of larger units under French protection – known as the Rheinbund or Confederation of the Rhine. Attempts by Prussia to impede this process merely accelerated it when she was defeated at Jena, and in 1807 an entirely new kingdom of Westphalia, including the British monarch's former electorate of Hanover, was created under the rule of the youngest Bonaparte brother, Jérôme.

Poland, partitioned out of existence in 1795 by the three powers which Napoleon defeated between 1805 and 1807, was recreated, mostly at Prussia's expense, as the Duchy of Warsaw. Its territory was expanded, this time from Austria's share, after the Wagram campaign in 1809. Finally, in 1810, the Netherlands, since 1806 the kingdom of Holland ruled by Louis Bonaparte, was annexed to the French Empire, along with the North Sea coast of Germany as far as Hamburg.

At its height in 1810–11, the Empire directly ruled by Napoleon comprised 130 departments and a population of around 44 million. Beyond its official frontiers lay a more informal outer empire of satellite states ruled by Napoleon's relatives: Joseph in Spain, Jérôme in Westphalia, Caroline as wife of the often-absent Murat in Naples, Elise in Tuscany, Joséphine's son Eugène as viceroy of Italy. Beyond them were the client states of rulers made kings by Napoleon, like the Rheinbund monarchs of Bavaria, Baden-Württemberg and Saxony. The King of Saxony also served as Duke of Warsaw, heading the recreated Polish state. All these monarchs knew they were there to do Napoleon's will. So, however reluctantly, did Emperor Francis of Austria and King Frederick William of Prussia, defeated enemies biding their time but seeing no immediate prospect of recovering independent power.

This Europe-wide empire and system of domination, often proclaimed by Napoleon and his propagandists as a recreation of the ninth-century empire of Charlemagne, was not the result of a preconceived plan. It came together by a series of contingencies. But Napoleon was very clear what he wanted from it, and his demands overturned far more than the dynastic claims of traditional rulers. The combined effect was nothing less than the destruction of the European old regime.

Five key policies (all beginning with C) formed the driving force of the Napoleonic Empire. First, contributions: all territories under direct or indirect rule from Paris were expected to yield revenue for imperial purposes. Ever since the first revolutionary incursions into the lands of foreign enemies, the native inhabitants had been required to pay for what was then called their 'liberation'. It was always a condition of peace treaties that lands turned into sister republics should contribute a proportion of their wealth for the purposes of the power which had created them. This principle did not change when they became the emperor's satellite kingdoms. Until they were defeated, enemy territories were stripped arbitrarily of whatever assets the French could lay their hands on. Once peace was concluded, they would be required to pay substantial indemnities. French troops would be quartered on their territories to guarantee compliance – and serve whatever strategic purpose Napoleon might have – and the occupied, not the French occupiers, would pay for their upkeep. Thus, between 1805 and 1811 the lands of defeated enemies contributed around 50 million francs in direct payments to France, with a further 148 million francs still owing. In the decade between 1803 and 1813, satellite territories paid out more than 382 million francs towards the upkeep of French garrisons.

Yet at the same time the tax bases of several of the major regions in Italy, Germany and Poland were eroded by the creation from 1806 onwards of *dotations*: hereditary endowments of lands and revenues for the exclusive benefit of important imperial figures such as members of the Bonaparte family, ministers and marshals. All this eased the fiscal burden on the core Empire at the expense of the periphery, and in the satellites it meant hefty tax increases. Sometimes – as in many of the *dotations* that were seldom if ever visited by their recipients – burdens were maintained despite traditional inefficiencies, so as not to disrupt the flow of revenues. Elsewhere, zealous French or French-inspired administrators sought to introduce new and more efficient taxes, levied with rationality and uniformity. Neither was ever fully achieved, and there were huge variations in how far fiscal modernisation took root. But by the time of Napoleon's downfall, there was no prospect of ever re-establishing the bewildering variety of taxes and collection methods that had existed before his time. Bureaucrats, whether they worked with the French or against them, had seen the clear advantages of the methods and principles pioneered under Napoleonic rule.

Nor were the contributions of Napoleon's client states to his imperial project measurable entirely in money. He himself set even more store by soldiers. Every state subdued or created by French power was expected to introduce conscription along French lines. Each was set a target size for a standing army. One of the main aims of creating the Rheinbund was to set up German states with the resources to put 63,000 men at Napoleon's disposal. Between 1805 and 1813 these foreign levies saved France almost 250 million francs. During that time, non-French auxiliaries played an increasingly important part in Napoleon's campaigns, culminating in 1812 when two thirds of the 600,000 men marching into Russia were not French.

Conscription was the second policy. Napoleon liked conscript armies: conscription, he thought, was a more rational way of recruiting than relying on the diverse and often dubious motivations of volunteers. Conscripted units were more homogeneous, and in newly created states they could be a school of common citizenship. Even his defeated enemies accepted this, and some saw French-imposed conscription as a weapon that might be turned one day against their oppressor. But, as in France, the able-bodied young men targeted by conscription hated it, as did their largely peasant families who depended on their labour. Draft-dodging and desertion, therefore, were an imperial as much as a French problem, shading into brigandage, banditry and, when French power began to ebb, open resistance. Only in the Duchy of Warsaw did Napoleon's puppet regime find it easy to recruit and retain men, but expatriate Poles had been serving in French armies ever since the partition of their country in 1795. In their native land, recreated by Napoleon, he was welcomed as a heroic liberator. Meanwhile, the cost of raising and maintaining standing armies, not to mention sending them into action at the emperor's whim, meant that none of the satellite states, already burdened with indemnities and paying for French garrisons, was ever able to establish order in its finances.

This was in spite of enjoying the same windfall as the French revolutionaries in 1790: the plunder of the Church, Napoleon's third policy. Napoleon had made the permanent loss of Church lands a precondition of negotiating the Concordat with the pope. This was not merely to reassure acquirers of former ecclesiastical property. He also believed that in a secular world the Church should enjoy no independent wealth or power. This conviction became even clearer in his treatment of the Church beyond France. The annexation of the left bank of the Rhine entailed the destruction of extensive prince-bishoprics and the dissolution of monasteries. Ecclesiastical states and monasteries beyond the Rhine were then used to compensate secular rulers dispossessed by the annexation; by 1803 in the last great decision of the moribund Reich, the secularisation of Church property was extended to the whole of Germany. This final initiative came from greedy German lay rulers rather than Napoleon, but it was entirely in line with his own thinking.

Napoleon was particularly scornful of monks and monasteries and had begun their wholesale dissolution during his first conquest of northern Italy. As soon as his rule was re-established there after Marengo, he demanded that the pope accept a concordat analogous to that of France, implying the confiscation of ecclesiastical property and the subjection of the Church to lay authority and priorities. After the throne of Naples passed to the Bonapartes in 1806, there followed the closure of 1,322 monasteries, and the pope was pressed to agree to a Neapolitan concordat. By the time the proposals arrived, Pope Pius VII was a captive in France, after the annexation to the Empire in 1809 of his own dominions, the last remaining ecclesiastical state. Rome itself was now subject to the original Concordat and with the same consequences: monasteries were closed, feast days and pious ceremonies were suppressed, charitable provision plummeted. Everywhere the depredations of French soldiers, openly contemptuous of the Church's traditional ways, compounded the outrage to pious populations whose cultural world had been turned upside down by Napoleonic demands.

Not least among the changes were the provisions on marriage enshrined in the Napoleonic Civil Code. Napoleon regarded the Code, his fourth key policy, as his proudest achievement and he was determined to extend what he saw as its benefits to all his satellites. It seemed obvious to him that the end it put to feudalism and serfdom, the introduction of more equal transmission of property, equality before the law, freedom of conscience and the secularisation of civil life would be universally welcome. But the clergy were outraged by the treatment of marriage as a civil contract, and by the Code's recognition of divorce.

These provisions had to be omitted in much of Italy when the Code was introduced there. The possibility of divorce also threatened marriage settlements, while partible inheritance undermined the entails by which elite groups had traditionally kept their family property together throughout much of southern Europe and Germany.

Inevitably, too, new laws and procedures meant new courts and reorganisation of the legal profession. Thus the introduction of the Code proceeded very unevenly and was far from complete outside France when the Empire collapsed. It was complicated wherever *dotations* were established, since these were entailed estates not subject to the ordinary law. In Napoleon's mind they did not conflict. 'Introduce the Civil Code at Naples,' he told Joseph in 1806:

and at the end of a few years all the fortunes not attached to you will be destroyed … it consolidates your power, since through it, everything not entailed falls, and the only great houses remaining are those you raise up … That is what made me advocate a Civil Code and led me to establish it.[24]

Yet there was an obvious mismatch between the Code's egalitarianism and the existence of privileged entails; and the contradictions in imperial policies did not end there. Once war with Great Britain resumed, the driving force of the whole Empire increasingly seemed to be the fifth key policy, the so-called Continental System of excluding British products from continental markets. The idea was to defeat the 'nation of shopkeepers' by cutting it off from its most lucrative markets. France therefore needed to seal off the entire European coastline. This was why the Italian peninsula was progressively brought under French control; why the attempt was made to take over Spain and Portugal; why Holland and the north German coastline were incorporated into the Empire. While the Balkans and Scandinavia could not be entirely insulated, France's allies and satellites could be committed to enforcing the ban on their own account by not trading in British goods.

The greatest triumph for this policy was the agreement by Russia, when peace was made between the two emperors at Tilsit in 1807, to join the blockade. For a time serious damage was done to the British economy by this policy, but the effect on continental consumers was just as profound. Deprived of imports from Britain, they were forced to turn to the more expensive products of France, while finding that their own exports faced exclusionary tariffs there.

Napoleon regarded the outer Empire primarily as a market for French goods and as a source of raw materials. 'My principle', he wrote, 'is *France first* ... if English commerce is supreme on the high seas, it is due to her sea power … as France is the strongest land power, she should claim commercial supremacy on the continent.'[25] No wonder inhabitants of the satellites saw the Continental System as one more form of exploitation. They responded by smuggling on a massive scale. To combat this, the number of imperial customs officers was steadily expanded, and troops were often called in to reinforce them. In what became known as the 'Customs Terror', huge public bonfires of impounded contraband were lit. And, as despairing consumers in the satellite states watched them go up in smoke, they knew that certain French products were being traded with Britain under special licences. In 1810 French grain helped to save the great maritime enemy from famine. The absurdity of this had convinced the Russians by the end of that year that a boycott so full of privileged exceptions for French interests was pointless. Their official withdrawal marked the moment when the Empire of Napoleon began to unravel.

7

Resistance

The cabinets of Europe have no ground for reproaching the French for co-operation in the destructive plans of the usurper, since they themselves made treaties with him ... The weakness and disunity of the continental powers have paralysed all efforts at resistance and conservation. They have more effectively contributed to the success of the common enemy than the forces available to him in his own states.

Marc-Antoine Jullien,
The Preserver of Europe, 1813[26]

Napoleon never had much trouble with the French. They owed him too much. He had brought the domestic upheavals and uncertainties of over a decade of revolution to an end. He had comprehensively defeated the nation's foreign enemies and expanded its territorial limits. Although the glorious general peace of 1802 soon broke down, for ten more years he continued to win spectacular victories and subject much of the continent to French rule. All this kept him popular. Unable to mobilise mass support against him, his isolated opponents were reduced to plotting assassination, or simply to private grumbling. His resolute control of the press and the theatre left them no other outlet, and any suspicious behaviour was closely monitored by a well-organised network of police spies established by Joseph Fouché.

Unless they threatened his life, Napoleon treated his known domestic opponents mildly. Purged legislators or sacked ministers were redeployed to less public roles. The wily foreign minister Talleyrand, dismissed by the Emperor as 'shit in a silk stocking' after he resigned in 1807 and began discreet moves to restrain his master's plans, continued to be consulted regularly. Rejectors of imperial patronage, like the liberal Lafayette or the royalist

Chateaubriand, were left in peace, though not unwatched. Incorrigible mischief makers, like the self-important salon hostess Germaine de Staël, were simply exiled from Paris.

Paris was always well garrisoned with reliable troops, as General Malet, who tried to mount a coup against the absent emperor in 1812, found to his cost. And Paris was never allowed to go hungry, whatever the conditions elsewhere: Napoleon knew from personal observation how the unruly capital had brought down the monarchy in 1792. The most widespread resistance was not political, but merely defiance of unpopular laws in the form of draft-dodging, desertion (officially called 'insubordination') or smuggling. Both shaded into more general criminality or banditry, but even these were less virulent in France than in the outer Empire.

Only in 1809 did a new focus of opposition emerge when the emperor quarrelled with the pope and annexed his territories. Pius VII responded by excommunicating Napoleon and those who obeyed him. The Church was once more torn apart, as the pope refused to confer spiritual powers on new bishops, and a number already in office refused to support the emperor against Pius. Napoleon raged that he would demote the pope to a mere bishop of Rome and remove the capital of the Church to Paris. He might have done as much if he had not been distracted in Russia.

Meanwhile, however, the quarrel with the pope undid one of the greatest achievements of the Concordat of 1801: it made possible once more an alliance between the Catholic Church and a Bourbon pretender. In 1810 a shadowy royalist network, the Knights of the Faith, was established, dedicated to a restoration of the legitimate dynasty. Managed by pious noblemen of old stock, its achievements were limited until foreign powers brought Napoleon down, but then it played some part in ensuring that it was the Bourbons who succeeded the emperor.

Even outside France, until 1808 no serious resistance to Napoleon seemed possible on the continent. Every power which opposed him militarily was smashed between 1805 and 1807. At the 'Erfurt Interview' in 1808 they all agreed not to impede his foray into the Iberian Peninsula. His initial aim there had been to close the ports of Portugal to the trade of its oldest ally, Great Britain. Spain was then a French ally and allowed Napoleon's troops to cross its territory. But factionalism at the Spanish court led to appeals for French arbitration over who should sit on the throne, Carlos IV or his son Fernando. Napoleon summoned both to Bayonne and bullied them into renouncing their respective claims in favour of his own brother.

He expected the same sort of acquiescence that Joseph had received in Naples. Instead, much of Spain exploded into anti-French revolt. Portugal followed. Barely crowned, King Joseph was driven out of Madrid and a French army was defeated at Bailén. A week later a British force began to disembark in Portugal, which the French were forced to evacuate. An outraged Napoleon decided to cross the Pyrenees in person with his best troops, reassured by the promises at Erfurt. But a successful campaign was cut short when news arrived of Austrian mobilisation. The example of Spanish resistance had shown that French armies were not invincible, and the Austrians hoped to stir up similar patriotic fervour in Germany to underpin a new campaign to curb Napoleon's ambitions.

But Germany, equally suspicious of Austria's ambitions, scarcely stirred. The result was the Battle of Wagram, where Austrian forces were once more crushed. A German revolt did occur in 1809, but was confined to the mountains of the Tyrol. Transferred from age-old Austrian rule after Austerlitz to France's faithful satellite Bavaria, the Tyrolese rose up in support of their old rulers but were abandoned by them after Wagram. Resistance flickered on into 1810, when French troops helped to reimpose Bavarian rule.

There was endemic banditry throughout central and southern Italy from 1809 onwards, mostly in reaction to conscription, new taxes and French-inspired pillage of the Church. Calabria, supplied and encouraged from British-controlled Sicily, was largely out of the control of King Joachim Murat for most of his seven-year reign (1808–15). None of this defiance was on the scale of what happened in Spain. There, the removal of the legitimate dynasty unleashed tensions and hatreds across the peninsula which only focused intermittently on the French invaders. Although French forces in Spain at their peak reached 260,000 men, repeated sorties by Wellington's forces from their Portuguese bridgehead prevented Napoleon's army from imposing systematic control on a vast and geographically fragmented country.

At the very moment when he seemed close to success in 1811, Napoleon began to draw off men for his invasion of Russia. He always refused to return to Spain, and without his towering presence French commanders showed no consistent co-operation against the low-intensity but brutal resistance of the guerrillas. This, then, was the 'Spanish ulcer', a constant drain and distraction on Napoleon's other policies, and a continuing inspiration to his other enemies of how he might be opposed. These enemies included Tsar Alexander. As war approached, the tsar warned the French ambassador, 'The Spaniards have often been beaten and they have neither yielded, nor submitted … [they] prove that it is lack of perseverance which has doomed all the states on which your master has made war.'[27]

Obvious targets for this criticism were the Austrians. Four times in twenty years they had found the resources and will to go to war against France. Four times Napoleon beat them in the field – but on three out of the four occasions (1797, 1800 and 1809) they might have fought on rather than rushing in panic to make a humiliating peace. Only when they were sure, from the summer of 1813, that a Russo-Prussian alliance was holding together and determined to bring Napoleon down did they commit themselves to the final struggle.

Nobody could say, by contrast, that the British did not persevere. They had pursued the war against the revolutionary republic until they had no continental allies left. Soon convinced that there was no living amicably with the ambitions of the restless First Consul, they broke the Peace of Amiens and relied on their naval power to protect themselves and confine him to the continent. The Battle of Trafalgar ensured that they could. While Napoleon's Continental System aimed to defeat them by stifling British trade with the continent, a British counter-blockade sought to stifle the continent's trade with the rest of the world.

This trade war brought serious disruption to the British economy in 1810–11 and led the following year to open conflict with the United States. There was widespread unrest in English manufacturing districts, for which the war was blamed. But control of the seas enabled the island state to seek out new overseas markets and set up smuggling entrepôts in the North Sea, the Baltic and the Mediterranean.

Napoleon hoped his blockade would drain the British government of money, but its credit was never dented, and it was able to offer cash subsidies to any power willing to oppose the emperor. There was never any serious or sustained support in Great Britain for peace with France, even when military disaster struck, as with a catastrophic attempt to help the Austrians with an invasion of the Netherlands in 1809. By then the British had found a more viable continental foothold in Portugal, from where their forces, five years later, were able at last to set foot on French soil.

Yet Spanish and Portuguese resistance, even with British support, could never by itself have brought Napoleon down. His real nemesis was Russia. He knew the perils of invading that vast territory. One of his military heroes was the 'Swedish Meteor' Charles XII, who had come to grief in the depths of the Ukraine in 1709. But Napoleon had defeated Russian armies three times and he resented the tsar's insistence on treating him only as an equal, if not an upstart.

Alexander thought the Tilsit agreement of 1807 had set up equal spheres of influence. He found, like others before him, that any agreement was seen by Napoleon as a mere springboard for further demands. The establishment of the Duchy of Warsaw, welcomed enthusiastically by the Poles, looked to be the recreation of a problem to Russia's west which the partition of 1795 had solved – especially when, after Austria's defeat in 1809, the duchy's territory was enlarged at Habsburg expense. Alexander had expected French help in a war against the Turks in the Balkans, but received none. A cherished uncle was dispossessed when the French Empire swallowed up territory around Hamburg. And when France began to license breaches of the Continental System while expecting Russia to boycott its long-standing British trading links, the tsar's patience snapped.

Both sides spent 1811 building up their forces. Napoleon forged a grand alliance of all his satellites as well as defeated enemies like Prussia and Austria, neither of whose leaders felt able to resist his demands. He planned an invasion with such overwhelming forces that the outcome of one good battle could never be in doubt. It was clear throughout Europe, as conscription intensified and supplies were stockpiled in eastern territories, that a new war was imminent, and the Russians were not taken by surprise. They made their own preparations. Although Francophobic Russian generals blustered about resisting invasion, the plan from the start was to let it happen, deny Napoleon his classic knockout battle and lure him ever further from his base into the heart of hostile territory. Only when he was approaching Moscow, with his forces depleted and worn down by marching across scorched earth in overwhelming heat or summer downpours, did the Russians feel they could and should make a stand.

On 7 September 1812 they did so at Borodino, the bloodiest battle that Napoleon had ever fought. There were 74,000 casualties. It was more like a draw than the clear French victory that Napoleon sought. As at Eylau, the Russians withdrew in reasonable order. They made no further attempt to defend Moscow, and the French took the city a week later. Napoleon now waited for Alexander to seek terms. Instead, the Russians set fire to their ancient capital.

After four weeks, with winter on the horizon, the shrunken French army began to withdraw. The cold came early and, as the tsar had foreseen, it ravaged the invaders as they retreated along a route already stripped of supplies by their earlier advance, mercilessly harassed by a hostile population and marauding Cossacks. Two months into the retreat, Napoleon left the remnants of his army and hastened back to Paris. In six months of campaigning in Russia the myth of his invincibility had been shattered – and the basis laid for his overthrow.

8

Downfall

The moment has arrived when you and Europe both throw down the gauntlet ... and it will not be Europe that will be defeated ... You are lost, Sire.

Metternich to Napoleon, 1813[28]

Napoleon travelled from Russia to Paris by coach and sledge. Once, he would have done it on horseback, but even before he invaded Russia it was widely observed that he was no longer the man he had been. He had grown plump. He ate more, relaxed more with his new wife and son, and also suffered from a growing number of debilitating ailments. Some discerned a growing inflexibility of mind, a tendency to wishful thinking, perhaps born of enjoying unchecked power for too long. He was still capable of spectacular bouts of energy, especially on campaign, but there were also more frequent spells of gloomy inertia and introspection.

Even before the Russian catastrophe, he had enough to preoccupy him beyond the everyday routines of government. A decade of economic good fortune was coming to an end. Poor harvests in 1810 and the following year brought rising food prices and a slump in demand for manufactures. To chronic unemployment in seaports blighted by the commercial war against Britain were added thousands of layoffs in hitherto revitalised centres of manufacture like Lyon and Paris itself. Businesses found themselves overstocked and unable to meet their debts. This in turn put banks under pressure, and credit dried up. Tax yields began to shrink, and throughout 1813, as the imperial grip on satellite and annexed territories weakened, they could not be supplemented as they had been for years by exactions from foreigners. More vigorous collection, as in the Customs Terror, merely intensified the recession by disrupting formerly flourishing black markets in contraband.

Only the supply of war materials continued to prosper, whether in the build-up to the invasion of Russia or restocking in its disastrous aftermath. Some resources could not be restored easily: while Russia had seemingly endless reserves of horses, Napoleon and his allies had lost 175,000 of their best mounts and draught animals. It was easier to replace men. The emperor returned to France determined to carry on the struggle, and by mid-April 1813 he had conscripted nearly half a million fresh soldiers. Many were very young, there was no time to train them properly, and there was a lack of experienced junior officers to do so. But the Russians were also exhausted by their struggle, and influential voices around the tsar urged him not to pursue the invaders beyond Russian territory. He brushed them aside. The opportunity of Napoleon's discomfiture, he thought, could be used to create lasting peace by pushing French power permanently back beyond the Rhine. He was encouraged by mounting defections of Prussian troops from their hated French alliance, and he confidently marched into Prussia, driving its French occupiers before him. In March the Russians entered Berlin and King Frederick William renounced the humiliating alliance that Napoleon had forced upon him. Thus began the German War of Liberation.

Within weeks the British had contacted the new allies with offers of financial subsidies. Yet the campaign of 1813 began well for Napoleon. Most of the Rheinbund states – his creations, after all – remained loyal to him and contributed troops. Although Austria now refused to fight alongside him, the Austrians did not intervene as he won a number of hard-fought battles. It came as a surprise when in May he agreed to an armistice. His troops were exhausted, and his victories, as always now, had cost him massive casualties. Even so, he later looked back on this truce as a fatal mistake. It revealed his weakness, it gave the allies time to regroup and it brought Austria into the war against him. Ostensibly it was arranged that a still-neutral Austria would offer mediation, but the peace terms proposed by the Austrian minister Metternich would have stripped France of much of the power it had achieved beyond the Rhine over the preceding dozen years. An outraged Napoleon rejected the terms – on the very day that news arrived of Wellington's decisive defeat of Joseph Bonaparte at Vitoria in Spain. The Austrian reaction was to join the allies. For the first time in the entire Napoleonic epic, all the great powers of Europe had come together against him.

It was an uneasy coalition, constantly stalked by mutual suspicion among the partners. If Napoleon had won another great battle it might well have fallen apart. But when fighting was resumed after the truce he was hugely outnumbered and outgunned. The allies deliberately avoided fighting him in person until their full resources were marshalled, but on 16–19 October they finally confronted him outside Leipzig in the 'Battle of the Nations'. It was the greatest battle ever fought in Europe up to that point. Forces numbering around 600,000 were involved, and casualties ran to 120,000. It was not the last of Napoleon's engagements but it was the decisive one. His power was broken. All his remaining allies deserted him, and by the end of the year he was out of Germany, leaving only a few isolated garrisons to be mopped up. Even now the allies offered him terms: peace and the 'natural' Rhine frontier achieved during the Revolution. He lost that chance by delaying a reply, and as 1814 began, Russian, Prussian and Austrian troops moved into French territory. British and Portuguese forces under Wellington had already been on the French side of the Pyrenees for some weeks.

Deeply divided as the allies were about what sort of France they wanted in the future, one by one they came to the conclusion that there could be no place in it for Napoleon. They took some trouble, in advance of their invasion, to proclaim to the French people that their quarrel was with him, not them. They remained apprehensive that their arrival on French soil would be met by a violent uprising in support of the emperor. In the event, they encountered very little popular resistance. The French were war-weary, sickened by relentless and ever-heavier conscription and staggering tax rises. The prospect of a rapid peace was perhaps a price worth paying for the first foreign invasion since 1792.

Yet Napoleon was determined to resist to the last, and in a few weeks of brilliant campaigning he defeated allied armies one by one, preventing them from consolidating their numerical advantage. Shaken, the invaders offered him peace again, though now on the basis of France's 'former limits'. But success, however desperate, always made Napoleon intransigent, and he spurned this last chance to keep his throne. The allies now committed themselves to restoring France's 'historic' frontiers, as they had been when Napoleon was still an unknown junior officer. This he could never accept. To settle for a France smaller than he had found it was, he declared, to break his coronation oath. More importantly, he feared that such a settlement would unleash a revolution of outrage in France which would bring him down. So he vowed to fight on.

Allied numbers and diplomatic determination now began to tell. In the south, Bordeaux welcomed the advancing Anglo-Portuguese army and ran up the white flag of the Bourbons. Napoleon manoeuvred frantically to prevent an allied convergence on Paris, but the marshals he despatched to protect the capital saw further resistance as fruitless. To the echo of gunfire from 100,000 allied troops, they surrendered the city. Napoleon's final march stalled 40 miles to the south, at Fontainebleau.

The emperor was abandoned by men who owed everything to him, and not only his generals. As the Russian tsar and the King of Prussia rode into Paris, Talleyrand, who had intrigued for years to restrain Napoleon, convened the Senate. With little hesitation this assembly of imperial superstars proclaimed the emperor's deposition. Napoleon tried to abdicate in favour of his son, but the allies would not hear of it. On 11 April 1814 he abdicated unconditionally, and the Senate invited Louis XVIII to take the vacant throne. The former master of Europe, unsuccessful in an attempt at suicide, was allowed to remain a ruler, but only of the tiny island of Elba.

These arrangements could not last. Elba was in effect a prison, and from the start many thought it would not be secure enough to hold Napoleon. They were right. Perturbed by persistent rumours of transfer to a remoter exile, resentful that the new French government was withholding the pension package he had been promised, the fretful exile was exhilarated to learn that the restored Bourbon monarchy was proving a disappointment. Although the king's constitutional 'Charter' vouchsafed the one thing Napoleon had never allowed, a truly representative legislature, back with the Bourbons came the old nobility and a militant Catholic Church, reviving the anxieties of those who had acquired lands. The end of the Continental System brought a renewed economic slump as cheap British goods flooded the market, while grandiose imperial public works were cancelled. Above all the army, whose needs had always been the first priority under the rule of a general, was ruthlessly slimmed down under his ostentatiously pacific successor. Military discontents were focused by the abandonment of the revolutionary tricolour under which the imperial army had marched to so much glory.

Napoleon's escape from Elba in March 1815 was an attempt to profit from these discontents. The very boldness of this 'Flight of the Eagle' awoke memories of more stirring times. His progress from the Mediterranean coast to Paris was greeted with popular enthusiasm. Seasoned soldiers sent to stop him refused to attack their former commander-in-chief. Napoleon knew, however, that not all of France welcomed his return. He tried to conciliate liberal opinion by promulgating an 'Additional Act to the Imperial Constitution', largely written by one of his most consistent critics since the days of the Consulate, Benjamin Constant. It promised representative government and guaranteed a range of civil rights – all things that Napoleon had always carefully avoided. It would have transformed the autocratic emperor into a constitutional monarch. It was endorsed by the first plebiscite since 1804 – but only days before Napoleon led a rejuvenated army north to confront British, Dutch and Prussian forces hurriedly massing in Belgium.

Ever since the abdication, representatives of the victorious allies had been in Congress at Vienna planning the post-war order in Europe. News of Napoleon's return from Elba alarmed but did not deter them. They simply declared him an international outlaw with whom they refused to deal. It seems improbable that if he had won at Waterloo he would have accepted the constraints of the Additional Act. It is equally improbable that allied solidarity against him would have buckled. Napoleon in power meant war without end. Waterloo removed that prospect, and when the defeated emperor returned to Paris he soon recognised that the support he had won during the 'Hundred Days' had evaporated. Within four days of the battle he abdicated again and, rather than face the vengeance of monarchs whose realms he had repeatedly ravaged, he threw himself on the mercy of the one enemy who had always been beyond his reach. He appealed to George, the British Prince Regent, for a dignified exile across the Channel. But the British, with the full support of their allies, had an altogether less comfortable island prepared for him.

9

Aftermath

Alive, the world eluded him, in death he possessed it ... having suffered the despotism of his person, we must now suffer the despotism of his memory.

Chateaubriand[29]

Napoleon spent his last six years in morose captivity on St Helena, a tiny inhospitable and rat-infested island in the tropical South Atlantic, thousands of miles from Europe. His main occupation, apart from bickering with the British governor whose orders were to treat him as a general but not an emperor, was boosting his historical reputation for posterity. He dictated memoirs. More importantly, he simply reminisced to a faithful inner circle who he knew were taking down his every word with a view to later publication.

Some of the conversations were not deciphered or published until the twentieth century, but two accounts of Napoleon's life and opinions in exile appeared shortly before he died of stomach cancer in 1821. Barry O'Meara, an Irish doctor assigned to him by the British military, offered English-speaking readers *Napoleon in Exile; or, a Voice from St Helena*, while Emmanuel de Las Cases, a convert from Bourbon legitimism who volunteered to join the fallen titan in exile, produced in French what rapidly became a bible of Bonapartism, the *Memorial of St Helena*.

Both were instant best-sellers. Las Cases' in particular was a masterpiece of propaganda. Exploiting the promethean pathos of the former master of Europe now confined to a remote and windswept rock, he painted his hero's downfall as a loss of promise. Never an aggressor, Napoleon had always acted in self-defence. A 'Prince of liberal ideas',[30] he had secured what was best in the work of the Revolution while ending its lethal chaos. He had been chosen by the nation for this work, and his true political instincts were embodied in the Additional Act of 1815 which, like earlier accretions to his power, had been overwhelmingly endorsed by plebiscite. His long-term ambition, Las Cases reported him as saying, was to unite Europe through common institutions, laws and currency. If he had sometimes acted tyrannically, it had always been not through inclination, but 'necessity'; and when he had fought, it had always been in self-defence.

Nobody had much direct information about Napoleon on St Helena until these accounts appeared. Yet the brief experience of the first Bourbon restoration and the Hundred Days had transformed his standing. Weary though most French people were of his warmongering ways and insatiable demands, they felt humiliated by Napoleon's defeat at the hands of foreigners whom French armies had previously brushed aside. The dismal experience of Bourbon rule united a whole spectrum of republicans and liberals in longing for the return of an emperor who in his heyday had despised them as much as they did him. After his second overthrow, when anyone who had rallied to him was subjected to discrimination, persecution and even to murder in a wave of 'White' terror, the exiled hero became a symbol and focus for subversion.

Rumours abounded that 'he' (the name did not need to be spelled out) had escaped and would be returning again. When he died, many refused to believe it. Others thought the British had poisoned him. A massive market arose in Napoleonic souvenirs and memorabilia.

Nor was this appetite confined to France. Although established governments and elites throughout Europe rejoiced in Napoleon's downfall, his achievements left admirers everywhere. Even the pope, whom he had bullied remorselessly, continued to commend his restoration of the altars after a godless revolution. Italian patriots praised the way he had opened their minds to the dream of unification. Poles, now mostly absorbed into Russia, idolised him for momentarily recreating their vanished state as the Duchy of Warsaw. Even in Great Britain there was grudging admiration for the military genius of 'Little Boney', while radicals and reformers praised the way he had overturned so many corrupt thrones. Wellington himself installed a colossal classical statue of his vanquished opponent in his London mansion. Petty German princelings whom the emperor had made kings did not renounce their crowns when he fell, and, like the Bourbons in France, did not overturn legal and administrative structures which he had imposed. They did too much to make government more effective for them to be abandoned. Military men, meanwhile, brooded endlessly on the lessons of Napoleon's campaigns in what was remembered until 1914 as the 'Great War'. They scarcely realised, until it was too late, that Napoleonic warfare had been the last refinement of an old pattern of conflict that would be made redundant by railways and industrialisation.

Nowhere did Napoleon cast a longer shadow than in France. Until the middle of the nineteenth century, most French adults could still remember the glories of the Empire. As late as 1857, 390,000 of his old soldiers were recorded as still living. Some placed hopes of a Bonaparte restoration in Napoleon's son, whom they called Napoleon II, living since 1814 with his Habsburg relatives in Vienna as the Duke of Reichstadt. But an attempt to recall him when Charles X abandoned the throne in 1830 was thwarted by the supporters of the junior Bourbon claimant Louis-Philippe, and a plot the next year to foment a military mutiny involving Louis Napoleon, son of Louis Bonaparte and Joséphine's daughter Hortense, passed practically unnoticed. In any case, Reichstadt died childless in 1832.

The 1830s saw a flood of memoirs and increasing numbers of literary evocations of the glory days. Louis-Philippe, restoring the tricolour last flown by Napoleon, was determined to recruit Bonapartist opinion in support of his July Monarchy. He completed the great triumphal arch on the summit of the Champs Elysées, less than half built when the emperor fell. Restoring the old palace of Versailles – the only former royal residence never occupied by Napoleon – as a museum of 'all the glories of France', he filled it with vast pictures of imperial victories. Above all, in 1840, he negotiated the repatriation of the emperor's remains from St Helena. The body was buried where it still lies, surrounded by the tombs of France's greatest military heroes, under the gilded dome of the Invalides, amid ceremonial pomp watched by vast crowds.

Louis Napoleon thought this might be the moment to reassert his own claims to the Bonapartist mantle. After an inglorious attempt to stage another military mutiny at Strasbourg in 1836, he had been exiled to America and penned a political manifesto, *On Napoleonic Ideas* (1839) which was largely a digest of Las Cases' book. Now the evident excitement caused by the news that his uncle's body was on the way home encouraged him to try again. But an attempt to emulate the 1815 'Flight of the Eagle' from a landing at Boulogne was a fiasco. He was arrested, tried and imprisoned. His Bonaparte relatives disowned him. For all the popular nostalgia generated by the 'return of the ashes', Bonapartism as a political cause seemed lost.

But Louis Napoleon persisted. From prison he continued to write pamphlets. With a flash of his uncle's boldness, eventually he escaped and took refuge in England. What rescued him from oblivion was the Revolution of 1848, bringing the downfall of Louis-Philippe. The new republican regime committed itself to electing a president by manhood suffrage. Encouraged by the example of his uncle's plebiscites, Louis Napoleon had always advocated a universal male franchise, and now his faith was vindicated. He stood for the presidency and won, with a massive majority. The declared aims of the 'prince-president' were those of the First Consul in 1799: to reconcile opposed parties and reassure property owners. 'The name of Napoleon', he declared, 'is itself a programme: it signifies domestically, order, authority, religion, popular welfare; externally, national dignity.'[31]

It also signified, soon enough, impatience with elected assemblies and term limits. The four-year presidency was non-renewable, and all attempts to extend it were thwarted in the legislature. The deadlock was broken, in true Napoleonic style, with a *coup d'état* in 1851, declaring martial law, dissolving the assembly and introducing an amended version of the consular constitution of 1799. The date chosen was the anniversary of the imperial coronation, and of the Battle of Austerlitz. There was widespread opposition, but the army obeyed a Bonaparte. There were several hundred deaths and thousands were deported. It was far from a bloodless takeover like the coup of Brumaire, but the new order won massive support in a plebiscite. It extended the prince-president's term to ten years, but this no more satisfied him than it had his uncle. As Napoleonic symbolism proliferated everywhere, in flags, public buildings, anniversaries and coinage, the ultimate precedent was soon followed. In November 1852 a second French Empire was proclaimed, its ruler no longer prince-president, but hereditary emperor, Napoleon III.

The Second Empire lasted eight years longer than the first. Massively endorsed by a further plebiscite, it sought to depict itself, like its earlier namesake, as saving the country from republican anarchy. It showered surviving veterans of Napoleonic wars with honours. It published an official version of Napoleon's correspondence (only superseded recently as a key historical source by a much fuller scholarly edition). Above all, Napoleon III sought to give France a role in the wider world commensurate with the memory of his uncle's achievements. The Empire, he always insisted, meant peace, and one thing he never shared with his uncle was military talent. Nevertheless, he pursued an adventurous and opportunistic foreign policy, conciliating the British unlike his uncle, but avenging his late disasters by inflicting modest defeats on the Russians in the Crimea and the Austrians in northern Italy.

Armed intervention in Mexico, however (while the United States was distracted by civil war), ended in disaster and humiliation; and the French army had not recovered when it was thrown into a war to prevent Prussia from absorbing the whole of Germany. In fact the conflict of 1870 precipitated just that. In a few months of fighting France went down to comprehensive defeat. Routed in the field, the emperor abdicated. The Second Empire was at an end. When peace was concluded in 1871, France was forced to sign away Alsace and Lorraine. And so Napoleon III's adventures, like those of his hero uncle, had left France territorially smaller than he had found it.

Bonapartism never recovered. Napoleon III died in exile. His son and heir was killed in British service in Africa. Their bodies have never been returned to France. True, the Duke of Reichstadt now lies beside his father in the Invalides, but this was a dubious gift to a defeated France from Hitler. A Bonaparte dynasty still exists in the line of Jérôme, one-time King of Westphalia. Bonapartes have intermarried with real royal houses, but they are without political ambitions.

Napoleon's appearance remains one of the most widely recognised in history. And in French political culture at least, powerful Napoleonic reflexes still exist. The Fifth Republic, founded in 1958 by a general after a *coup d'état*, enshrines a powerful president directly elected by universal suffrage, enjoying democratic legitimacy at least equal to that of the National Assembly. This constitution, and periodic changes made to it, have been approved by plebiscites. When, on 14 July each year, the president reviews the armed forces, he is escorted from the Arc de Triomphe down the Champs Elysées by the mounted Republican Guard in Napoleonic uniforms – direct descendants of the emperor's most treasured troops.

The social, political and cultural history of France in the nineteenth century and beyond would have been quite different if Napoleon had never existed. His legacy in the rest of Europe was patchier but still profound. His Civil Code still forms the basis of much continental law. He shook Italy and Germany out of institutional inertia so thoroughly that they could never be reconstituted on the old basis after he fell. Ecclesiastical states disappeared for ever, apart from that of the pope. Even that only survived for a few decades, although the Catholic Church emerged reinvigorated from its struggle against a ruler who firmly believed that 'the empire of the Church was not of this world'.[32]

Beyond Europe, it seems likely that even if Napoleon had never existed, sooner or later Egypt would have been lost by the Ottomans, western expansion of the United States would have become unstoppable and the Iberian empires of Latin America would break away. Yet all these developments began with policy decisions taken by him. Momentous, too, was his decision to fight Great Britain by economic warfare rather than invasion. It lay behind his quarrel with the pope and his disastrous forays into Spain and Russia. And yet the British, impregnable behind their navy's 'wooden walls', used the struggle finally to consolidate the world economic and commercial hegemony towards which they had been moving for a century, and would enjoy for another. Even Napoleon's failures and mistakes, then, had enormous consequences.

Although he made himself a hereditary emperor and married a daughter of Europe's most distinguished dynasty, Napoleon called himself a son of the Revolution. He knew his career would have been impossible without it, and that his continued domestic success depended on consolidating its practical achievements while binding the wounds which it had opened. He always fought under its flag. France has never ceased to argue over the significance of an authoritarian adventurer with contempt for representative institutions. Were glory, plunder and 'order' enough to compensate for the loss of liberty? These questions still echo, as they did for one of his veterans:

We hated his despotism, but we could not but recognise in Napoleon an extraordinary Genius, which ultimately gave him the right to command and to be obeyed. In our eyes, he was one of those giants who emerge once every thousand years.[33]

Notes

1 Quoted in Herold, J. Christopher, *The Mind of Napoleon* (New York, 1955), p. 7.

2 Quoted in Chandler, David, *The Campaigns of Napoleon* (London, 1966), p. 53.

3 *Mémoires du Comte Miot de Mélito* (Paris, 1873), vol. 1, pp. 154, 184.

4 Pascal, François (ed.), *Antoine Claire Thibaudeau, Mémoires sur le Consulat 1799–1804* (Paris, 2013), p. 205.

5 Las Cases, Emmanuel de, *Le Mémorial de Sainte-Hélène*, 27 October 1816.

6 Montholon, C.J.T. de, *Récits de la Captivité de l'Empereur Napoléon à Sainte-Hélène* (Paris, 1847), vol. 2, p. 340.

7 Cited in Dwyer, Philip, *Napoleon: The Path to Power 1769–1799* (London, 2007), p. 198.

8 Quoted in Herold, *Mind of Napoleon*, p. 263.

9 Chaptal, Jean-Antoine, *Mes Souvenirs sur Napoléon* (Paris, 1893, new edn 2007), p. 88.

10 Fleuriot de Langle, Paul (ed.), *Général Bertrand: Cahiers de Sainte-Hélène, 1818–1819* (Paris, 1959), p. 428.

11 Speech in the House of Commons, 3 February 1800.

12 Quoted in Howard, John Eldred, *Letters and Documents of Napoleon, I: The Rise to Power* (London, 1961), pp. 367–8.

13 Bonaparte, Napoléon, *Correspondance Générale*, vol. 2 (Paris, 2005), p. 1122, no. 4826.

14 Bonaparte, Napoléon, *Correspondance Générale*, vol. 1 (Paris, 2004), p. 1081, no. 1822.

15 Pascal, *Antoine Claire Thibaudeau*, p. 55.

16 Quoted in Gaubert, Henri, *Conspirateurs au Temps de Napoléon 1er* (Paris, 1962), p. 235.

17 Quoted in Collins, Irene, *Napoleon and his Parliaments*,

1800–1815 (London, 1979), p. 115.

18 Montholon, *Récits*, vol. 2, pp. 240–1.

19 Earl Stanhope, *Notes of Conversations with the Duke of Wellington, 1831–1851* (London, 1886, new edn 1998), p. 76.

20 Ibid., p. 60.

21 Quoted in Longford, Elizabeth, *Wellington: The Years of the Sword* (St Albans, 1971) p. 318.

22 For this version of this famous remark, see Müchler, Günter, *Napoléon/Metternich: Le Jour où l'Europe a Basculé, Dresde, 26 Juin 1813* (Paris, 2013), pp. 253, 269–70, 300.

23 Stanhope, *Conversations with Wellington*, p. 76.

24 Haegele, Vincent (ed.) *Napoléon et Joseph Bonaparte. Correspondance intégrale 1784-1818* (Paris, 2007), p. 224.

25 Thompson, J. M. (ed.) *Letters of Napoleon* (Oxford, 1935), p. 274.

26 Quoted in Palmer, R.R., *From Jacobin to Liberal: Marc-Antoine Jullien, 1775–1848* (Princeton, 1993), p. 117.

27 Hanoteau, Jean (ed.), *Mémoires du Général de Caulaincourt, Duc de Vicence, Grand Ecuyer de l'Empereur* (Paris, 1933), vol. 1, p. 292.

28 Quoted in Esdaile, Charles, *Napoleon's Wars: An International History, 1803–1815* (London, 2007), pp. 505–6.

29 Chateaubriand, René de, *Mémoires d'Outre-Tombe*, (Paris, 1849), bk 24, ch. 8.

30 Las Cases, *Mémorial*, 19 December 1815.

31 Quoted in Hazareesingh, Sudhir, *The Legend of Napoleon* (London, 2004), p. 223.

32 Griffiths, Ralph A. (ed.) *In Conversation with Napoleon Bonaparte: J.H. Vivian's Visit to the Island of Elba* (Newport, 2008), p. 55.

33 Quoted in Hazareesingh, *Legend of Napoleon*, p. 257.

Timeline

A Note on the Revolutionary Calendar

The Revolutionary Calendar was officially operative from late 1793 until 1806. It began with the proclamation of the Republic in September 1792. The year was then divided into twelve thirty-day months named after the seasons, e.g. Thermidor (heat – July/August), Fructidor (fruiting – August/ September), Vendémiaire (harvesting – September/October), Brumaire (mists – October/ November).

1769	15 August: Napoleon born, Ajaccio, Corsica
1778	Sent to Brienne Military Academy, France
1785	Graduates from Military School in Paris
	Lieutenant of artillery
1789	Outbreak of French Revolution
1791	Back in Corsica
1792	In Paris when monarchy falls
1793	Family flees Corsica
	Siege of Toulon
1794	Briefly arrested after fall of Robespierre
1795	Writes *Clisson et Eugénie*
	Crushes uprising of Vendémiaire

1796	Marries Joséphine; commander in Italy
1797	Wins Italian campaign
	Coup of Fructidor
1798	Egyptian expedition
1799	Return from Egypt
	Takes power in coup of Brumaire
	First Consul
1800	Austrians defeated at Marengo
1801	Concordat with Catholic Church
1802	Peace of Amiens
	Consulate for life
	Failure of Haiti expedition
1803	Louisiana sold to United States
	War with Britain resumes
1804	Civil Code
	Kidnap of Enghien
	Napoleon crowns himself emperor
1805	Naval defeat at Trafalgar
	Austro-Russians defeated at Austerlitz
	Continental System inaugurated
1806	Prussians defeated at Jena
1807	Eylau, Friedland
	Treaty of Tilsit with Russia
	Duchy of Warsaw created
1808	Erfurt Interview
	Invasion of Iberia
	Imperial nobility established
1809	Austrians defeated at Wagram
	Joséphine divorced

1810	Napoleon I marries Marie-Louise
1811	King of Rome born
	Empire reaches its territorial peak with annexation of Holland and north Germany
1812	Invasion of Russia and retreat from Moscow
1813	German War of Liberation
	Defeat at Battle of the Nations at Leipzig
1814	Campaign of France
	Abdication
	Exile to Elba
1815	'Flight of the Eagle'
	The Hundred Days
	Final defeat at Waterloo
	Transfer to St Helena
1821	5 May: Napoleon dies on St Helena
1840	'Return of the Ashes', repatriation of Napoleon's body
1848	Louis Napoleon Bonaparte elected president of France
1852	Second Empire established under Napoleon III
1870	Abdication of Napoleon III after defeat in Franco-Prussian War
1873	Death of Napoleon III
1879	Death of Prince Imperial

Further Reading

Much of the most important material on Napoleon is available only in French. Books on Napoleon run into thousands. A few of the most useful, available in English, are listed here:

Alexander, Robert, *Napoleon* (London, 2001)

Bell, David A., *The First Total War: Napoleon's Europe and the Birth of Modern Warfare* (London, 2007)

Bergeron, Louis, *France under Napoleon* (Princeton, 1981)

Broers, Michael, *Europe under Napoleon, 1799–1815* (London, 2nd edn 2015)

Broers, Michael, *Napoleon, Soldier of Destiny* (London, 2014)

Carrington, Dorothy, *Napoleon and his Parents: On the Threshold of History* (London, 1988)

Chandler, David, *The Campaigns of Napoleon* (London, 1966)

Connelly, Owen (ed.), *Historical Dictionary of Napoleonic France* (London, 1985)

Connelly, Owen, *Blundering to Victory. Napoleon's Military Campaigns* (Wilmington, 1987)

Dwyer, Philip, *Napoleon, 1, The Path to Power, 1769-1799* (London, 2007)

Ellis, Geoffrey, *The Napoleonic Empire* (Basingstoke, 2nd edn, 2003)

Emsley, Clive, *The Longman Companion to Napoleonic Europe* (London, 1993)

Englund, Stephen, *Napoleon: A Political Life* (New York, 2004)

Esdaile, Charles, *Napoleon's Wars. An International History, 1803–1815* (London, 2007)

Forrest, Alan, *Napoleon* (London, 2011)

Gates, David, *The Napoleonic Wars, 1803–1815* (London, 1997)

Geyl, Pieter, *Napoleon: For and Against* (London, 1949)

Herold, J. Christopher, *The Mind of Napoleon: A Selection from his Words* (New York, 1955)

Hazareesingh, Sudhir, *The Legend of Napoleon* (Oxford, 2004)

Holtman, Robert B. *The Napoleonic Revolution* (Philadelphia, 1967)

Howard, John Eldred, *Letters and Documents of Napoleon, Vol.1: The Rise to Power* (London, 1961)

Jordan, David P., *Napoleon and the Revolution* (Basingstoke, 2012)

Lieven, Dominic, *Russia against Napoleon: The Battle for Europe, 1807–1814* (London, 2009)

Markham, Felix, *Napoleon* (Oxford, 1963)

Price, Munro, *Napoleon: the End of Glory* (Oxford, 2014)

Rapport, Mike, *The Napoleonic Wars: A Very Short Introduction* (Oxford, 2013)

Roberts, Andrew, *Napoleon the Great* (London, 2014)

Rothenburg, Gunther, *The Art of Warfare in the Age of Napoleon* (London, 1977)

Schroeder, Paul W., *The Transformation of European Politics, 1763–1848* (Oxford, 1994)

Smith, William H., *The Bonapartes: the History of a Dynasty* (London, 2005)

Thompson, J.M., *Letters of Napoleon* (Oxford, 1934)

Tulard, Jean, *Napoleon. The Myth of the Saviour* (Oxford, 1984)

Woloch, Isser, *Napoleon and his Collaborators. The Making of a Dictatorship* (New York, 2001)

Woolf, Stuart, *Napoleon's Integration of Europe* (London, 1991)

Web Links

www.napoleon.org – Official website of the Fondation Napoléon, the leading centre for the study of all things Napoleonic. Offers guidance on sources and further research as well as current events and publications. In French, but electronically translatable

www.napoleonguide.com – A vast miscellany of snippets, both important and trivial, including current events, anniversaries, sales, books and pictures

www.napoleon-series.org – Website sponsored by the International Napoleonic Society. Another miscellany, with strong military bias. Interactive discussions

www.NapoleonicSociety.com – Website of the International Napoleonic Society. A full range of links, references and reviews

www.napoleonicassociation.org – A website for war-gamers and re-enactors

www.fsu.edu/napoleon – Website of the Institute on Napoleon and the French Revolution of Florida State University, the leading American centre for Napoleonic studies

Giuseppe Verdi Henry V **Brunel** Pope John Paul II **Jane Austen** William the Conqueror **Abraham Lincoln** Robert the Bruce **Charles Darwin** Buddha **Elizabeth I** Horatio Nelson **Wellington** Hannibal & Scipio **Jesus** Joan of Arc **Anne Frank** Alfred the Great **King Arthur** Henry Ford **Nelson Mandela**